Contents

Formula Sheet

Exam 1

Paper 1A — calculator paper 1
Paper 1B — non-calculator paper 17

Exam 2

Paper 2A — calculator paper 33
Paper 2B — non-calculator paper 49

Answers 65

Published by Coordination Group Publications Ltd.
Contributors:
Charley Darbishire Andy Park
Simon Little Glenn Rogers
Iain Nash Claire Thompson
ISBN: 1-84146-026-5
Groovy website: www.cgpbooks.co.uk
Printed by Elanders Hindson, Newcastle-upon-Tyne.
Occasional bits of clipart from CorelDRAW
Text, design, layout, and original illustrations © Coordination Group Publications Ltd. 2001
All rights reserved.

GCSE Mathematics
Formulae Sheet: Intermediate Tier

Area of trapezium = $\frac{1}{2}(a+b)h$

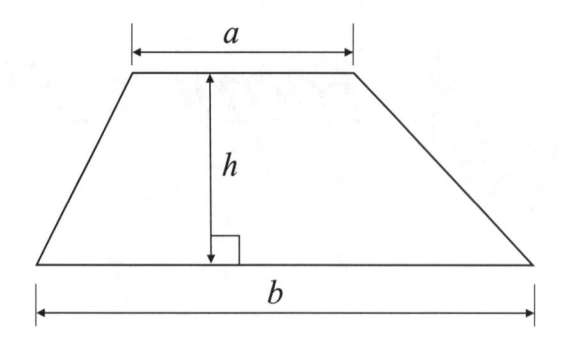

Volume of prism = area of cross section × length

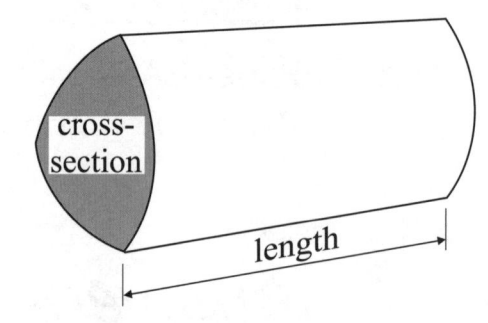

CGP Practice Exam Paper — GCSE Mathematics

General Certificate of Secondary Education

GCSE
Mathematics
Paper 1A – calculator paper

Intermediate Tier

Centre name

Centre number

Candidate number

Surname

Other names

Candidate signature

Time allowed: 2 hours.

In addition to this paper you may need:
- A ruler.
- A protractor.
- A pair of compasses.
- An electronic calculator.
- Tracing paper may be used.

Instructions to candidates
- Write your name and other details in the spaces provided above.
- Answer **all** questions in the spaces provided.
- Do all rough work on the paper.
- Take the value of π to be 3.142, or use the π button on your calculator.

Information for candidates
- The marks available are given in brackets at the end of each question or part-question.
- You may get marks for method, even if your answer is incorrect.
- In calculations show clearly how you work out your answers.
- You are expected to use a calculator where appropriate.
- There are 20 questions in this paper. There are no blank pages.

Advice to candidates
- Work steadily through the paper.
- Don't spend too long on one question.
- If you have time at the end, go back and check your answers.

For examiner's use

Q	Attempt Nº 1	2	3	Q	Attempt Nº 1	2	3
1				12			
2				13			
3				14			
4				15			
5				16			
6				17			
7				18			
8				19			
9				20			
10							
11				Total 100			

© 2001 CGP

1 (a) Draw an enlargement of this shape on the grid. Use a scale factor of 3.

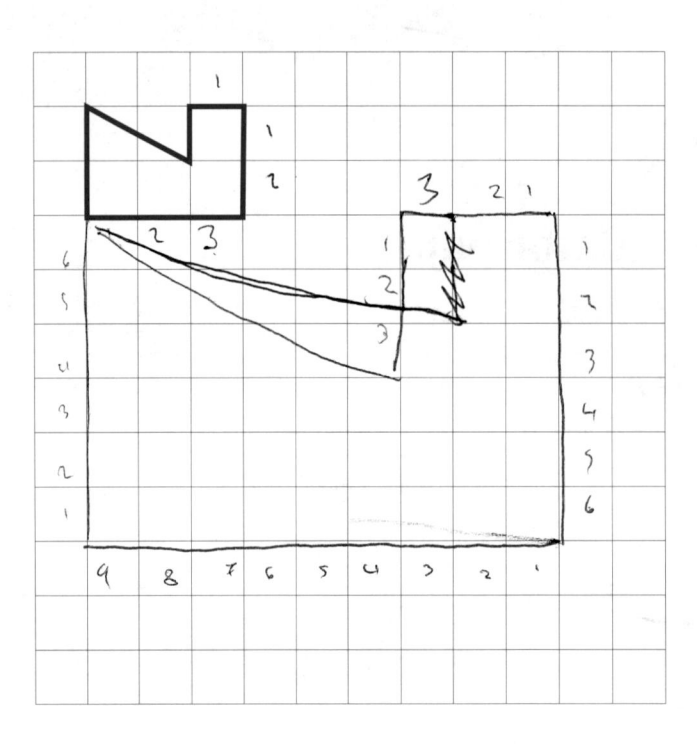

(2 marks)

(b) Calculate the volume of this cuboid.

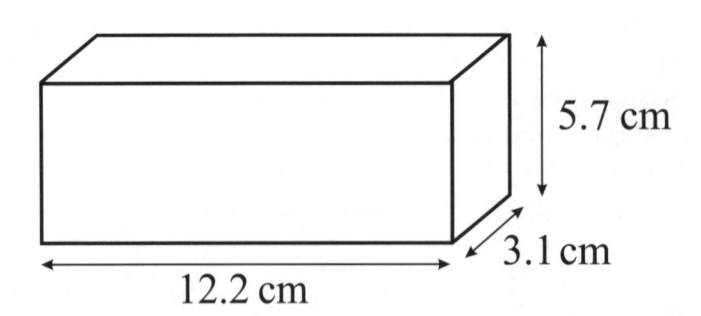

....

....

....

Answer (b) _____ cm³

(2 marks)

2   Use your calculator to find the value of

$$\frac{\sqrt{11.4-2.9^2}}{8.1} \times 0.72$$

Give your answer correct to 1 decimal place.

....

....

....

Answer _____

(3 marks)

3   Calculate the area of this triangle.

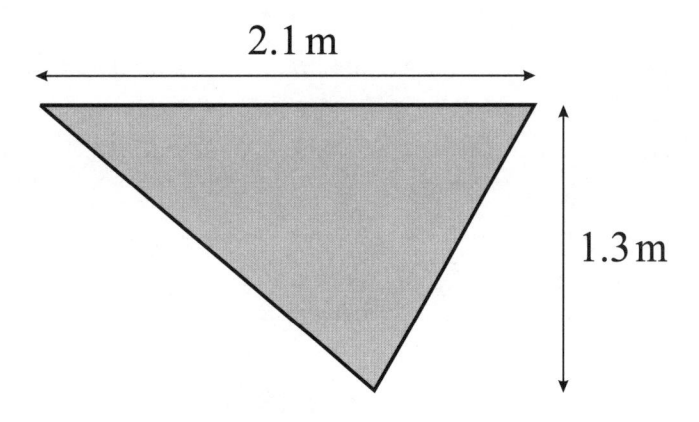

....

....

....

Answer _____ m²

(2 marks)

4   (a) Rhonda buys   2.1 kg apples
                          700 g carrots
                          3 pumpkins

Pumpkins £1.70 each
Apples £1.14 per kg
Carrots 78p per kg
Bananas £1.99 per kg
Oranges £1.53 per kg

How much change does she get from £20? Show your calculations.

....

....

....

....

Answer (a) _____

(4 marks)

98p — Juicy Juice 1 litre
81p — FRESH N' JUICY 750 ml

(b) Which of these cartons of orange juice is better value for money?
     Show how you make your decision.

....

....

....

Answer (b) _____

(2 marks)

SALE 14% OFF MARKED PRICES   £36.99

(c) Rhonda bought this dress in a sale. How much did it cost?

....

....

....

Answer (c) _____

(3 marks)

5   To make concrete, you need to use cement, sand and water in the ratio
     Cement : Sand : Water = 1 : 3 : 2

   (a) How much sand is needed with $3\frac{1}{2}$ kg of cement?

   ....

   ....

   Answer (a) _____ kg
   (2 marks)

   (b) If I want to have 20 kg of concrete, how much sand will I need?

   ....

   ....

   Answer (b) _____ kg
   (2 marks)

6   A sports club buys an exercise bike. The club is given a discount of $\frac{1}{16}$ of the price.

   (a) Write $\frac{1}{16}$ as

     (i) a decimal,

     Answer (a) (i) _____

     (ii) a percentage.

     Answer (a) (ii) _____ %
     (2 marks)

   The normal price of the exercise bike is £369.

   (b) Calculate the price the sports club had to pay for the exercise bike.

   ....

   ....

   Answer (b) £_____
   (3 marks)

7 A group of 20 lengths in metres of a box of ropes is recorded.

36.1	25.8	15.8	8.9
22.7	34.1	5.6	33.0
45.6	24.6	1.4	35.9
7.1	3.5	24.6	14.5
1.8	16.4	4.4	9.2

(a) Complete the frequency table, using intervals of 10 metres.

Length (l) metres	Tally	Frequency
$0 \leq l < 10$		

(3 marks)

(b) Write down the modal class interval.

Answer (b) _____

(1 mark)

8 The equation
$$x^2 - 2x = 4$$
has a solution between 3 and 4.
Use a trial and improvement method to find this solution.
Give your answer correct to 1 decimal place.
You must show ALL your working.

Answer $x =$ _____

(4 marks)

9   Beth asked 90 musicians what instrument they played.
    Here are her results.

Instrument	Piano	Guitar	Flute	Accordion	Tuba
Number of musicians	33	21	18	5	13

(a) Draw a pie chart to show these results.

(3 marks)

Beth also asked 180 people about the pets they owned.
In a pie chart showing the results, the angle for dogs was 128°.

(b) How many of these people said that they owned a dog?

....

....

....

Answer (b) _____

(2 marks)

10

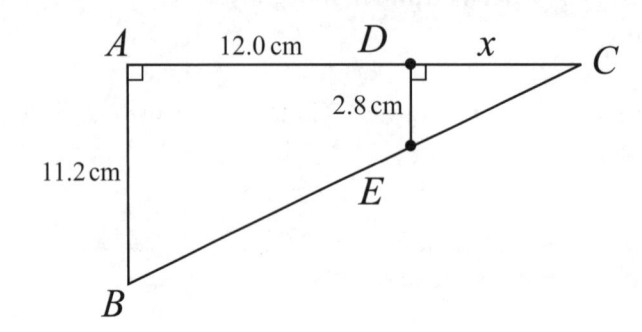

ABC is a right-angled triangle.

DE is parallel to *AB*.

AB = 11.2 cm,   *DE* = 2.8 cm,   *AD* = 12.0 cm.

(a) Calculate the area of the trapezium *ADEB*.

Answer (a) _____ cm²
(2 marks)

CD = *x* cm.

(b) Calculate the value of *x*.

Answer (b) *x* = _____
(3 marks)

11 (a) *ABCDE* is a regular pentagon with centre *O*.

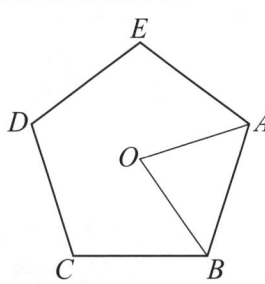

(i) Calculate the angle *AOB*. Show your working.

....

....

Answer (a) (i) _____

(2 marks)

(ii) Calculate angle ABC. Show your working.

....

....

Answer (a) (ii) _____

(2 marks)

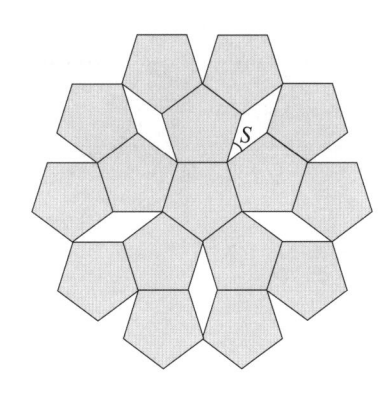

(b) The diagram shows part of a tiled floor. The grey tiles are regular pentagons. Calculate the angle marked *S*.

....

....

....

Answer (b) _____

(2 marks)

12 Simplify

(a) $x + x + x + x + x$

Answer (a) _____
(1 mark)

(b) $2y + 5y - 4y + 6y - y$

Answer (b) _____
(2 marks)

13 (a) Expand and simplify

$(x - 7)(x + 2)$

Answer (a) _____
(1 mark)

(b) Factorise completely

$2x^2 + 6xy$

Answer (b) _____
(2 marks)

14

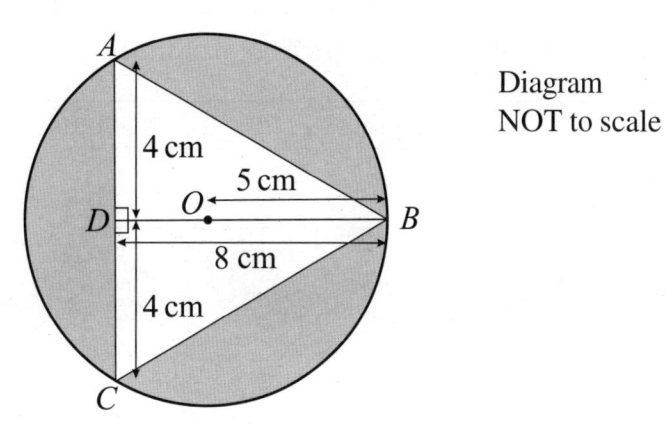

Diagram NOT to scale

The diagram shows two identical right-angled triangles inside a circle.
A, B and C are points on the circumference of the circle.
The radius of the circle OB is 5 cm.
AD = DC = 4 cm and BD = 8 cm.

Work out the area of the shaded part of the circle.
Give your answer correct to the nearest cm².

Answer _____ cm²

(6 marks)

15 Abdul recorded the lap times of people on a go-kart track at a theme park.
This is his table showing the grouped distribution of times.

Time (s seconds)	$0 < s \leq 10$	$10 < s \leq 20$	$20 < s \leq 30$	$30 < s \leq 40$	$40 < s \leq 50$	$50 < s \leq 60$
Number of people (frequency)	5	12	37	19	9	2

(a) (i) Write down the modal class.

Answer (a) (i) _____

(1 mark)

(ii) On the grid below draw a frequency polygon representing the distribution.

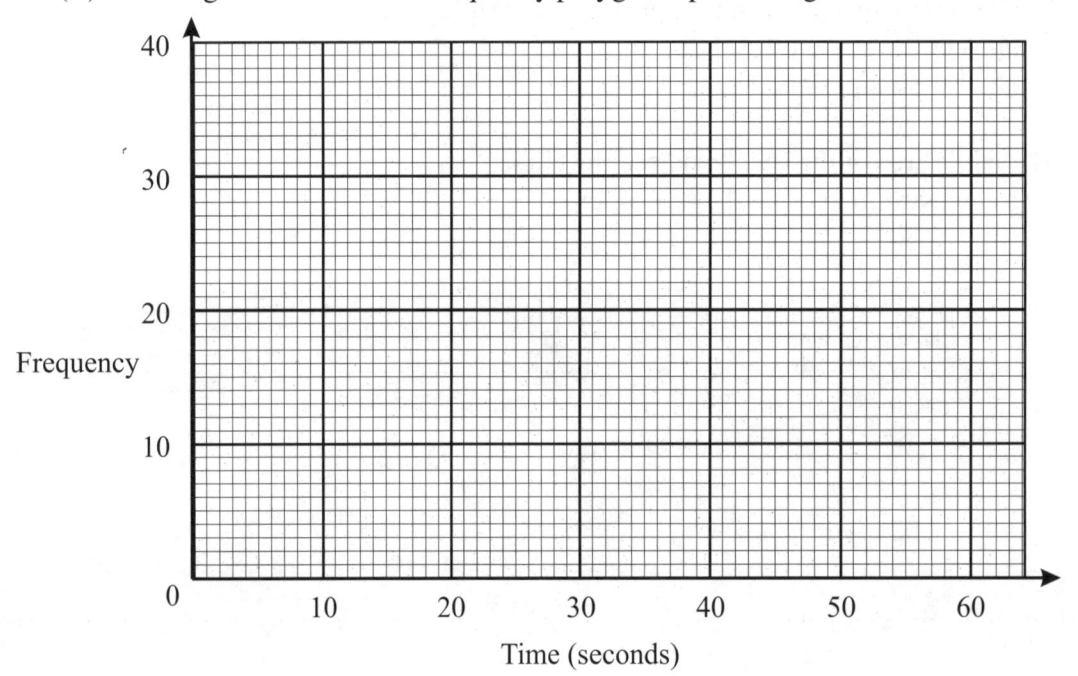

(3 marks)

(b) Calculate an estimate of the mean lap time of the people at the theme park.

Answer (b) _____ seconds

(4 marks)

16   1 kg = 2.2 pounds
      1 tonne = 10^3 kg

(a) How many kg are equal to $\frac{1}{10}$ pound?

Write your answer in standard form correct to 3 significant figures.

....

....

Answer (a) _____

(3 marks)

A lorry carries 2 tonnes when it is 60% full.

(b) What is the maximum carrying capacity of the lorry in pounds?
Give your answer correct to 3 significant figures.

....

....

Answer (b) _____

(3 marks)

17

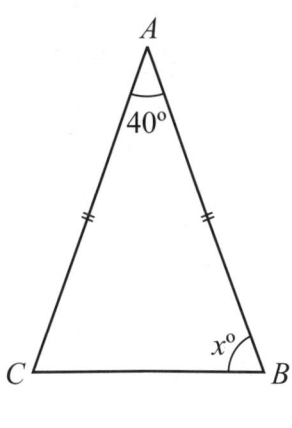

In triangle ABC,
$AB = AC$, and angle $CAB = 40°$.

(a) Write down the special name for triangles like this one.

Answer (a) _____

(1 mark)

(b) Calculate the value of x.

....

....

Answer (b) x = _____

(2 marks)

18 The scatter graph shows information about the heights of six fathers and their sons.

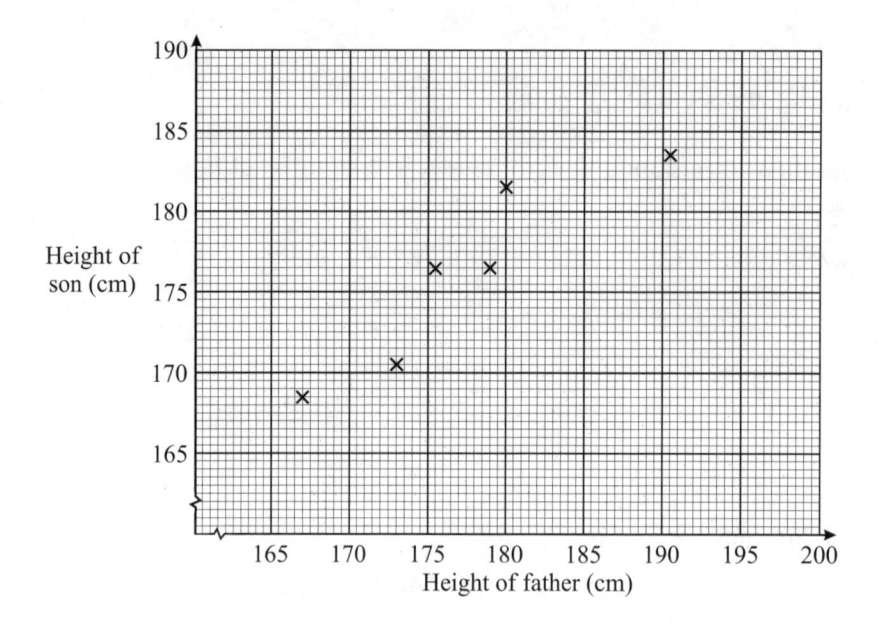

The table below shows the heights of five more fathers and their sons.

Height of father (cm)	163	185	185	193	197
Height of son (cm)	167	180	187	188	182

(a) Plot the information from the table on the scatter graph.

(2 marks)

(b) Briefly describe the relationship between the heights of the fathers and the heights of the sons.

Answer (b) _____

_____

(1 mark)

(c) Draw a line of best fit on the scatter graph.

(2 marks)

The height of another man is 175 cm.

(d) Use your line of best fit to give an estimate of the height of his son.

Answer (d) _____ cm

(1 mark)

A different man is 184 cm tall.

(e) Use your line of best fit to estimate the height of his father.

Answer (e) _____ cm

(1 mark)

19

5x + 7

3x

The diagram shows a rectangle of length 5x + 7 and height 3x, where all measurements are in metres.
The perimeter of the rectangle is *P* metres.
The area of the rectangle is *A* square metres.

(a) Write down an expression in its simplest form, in terms of *x*, for

(i) *P*,

....

Answer (a) (i) _____

(ii) *A*.

....

Answer (a) (ii) _____

(3 marks)

P = 78.

(b) Work out the value of *A*.

....

....

....

Answer (b) _____

(3 marks)

20 (a)   1,   4,   13,   40, ...

You can find the next number in this sequence using the rule
   'Multiply the number by three and then add 1'.

(i) Calculate the next number in the sequence.

....

Answer (a) (i) _____
(1 mark)

(ii) A number later in the sequence is represented by *x*.
Write down the term in the sequence that comes after *x*.

....

Answer (a) (ii) _____
(2 marks)

The first rule was
   'Multiply the number by three and then add 1'.
(iii) Describe in words a different rule for continuing the sequence.

Answer (a) (iii) _____

_____
(2 marks)

(b) The first five terms of a different sequence are shown in this table.

Number of term (*n*)	1	2	3	4	5
Term	0	3	8	15	24

Find, in terms of *n*, an expression for the *n*th term of the sequence.

....

....

Answer (b) _____
(2 marks)

General Certificate of Secondary Education

GCSE
Mathematics
Paper 1B – non-calculator paper

Intermediate Tier

Time allowed: 2 hours.

| Centre name |
| Centre number |
| Candidate number |

| Surname |
| Other names |
| Candidate signature |

In addition to this paper you may need:
- A ruler.
- A protractor.
- A pair of compasses.
- Tracing paper may be used.

Instructions to candidates
- Write your name and other details in the spaces provided above.
- Answer **all** questions in the spaces provided.
- Do all rough work on the paper.

Information for candidates
- The marks available are given in brackets at the end of each question or part-question.
- You may get marks for method, even if your answer is incorrect.
- In calculations show clearly how you work out your answers.
- There are 18 questions in this paper. There are no blank pages.

Advice to candidates
- Work steadily through the paper.
- Don't spend too long on one question.
- If you have time at the end, go back and check your answers.

For examiner's use

Q	Attempt Nº 1	2	3	Q	Attempt Nº 1	2	3
1				12			
2				13			
3				14			
4				15			
5				16			
6				17			
7				18			
8							
9							
10							
11							
				Total 100			

© 2001 CGP

1 A tiled floor uses tiles that are these 3 shapes.

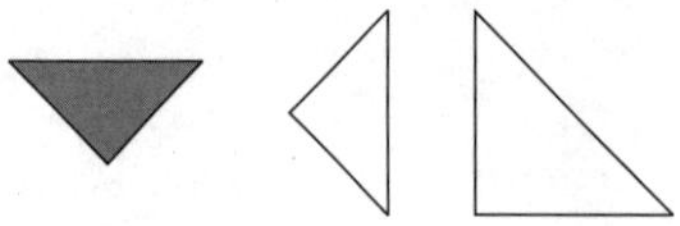

   Complete this floor design so that it has rotational symmetry.

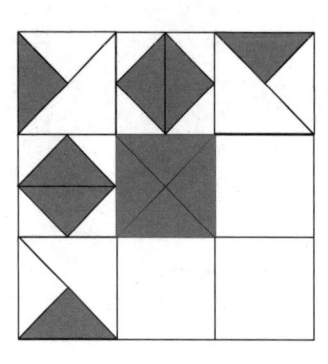

   (3 marks)

2 (a) Simplify $5x + 7y - x - 2y + 2x$.

   ....

   Answer (a) _____
   (2 marks)

   (b) Solve the equations

   (i) $3(2x - 5) = 9$

   ....

   ....

   ....

   Answer (b) (i) $x =$ _____
   (3 marks)

   (ii) $9x - 15 = 4x$

   ....

   ....

   ....

   Answer (b) (ii) $x =$ _____
   (2 marks)

3   When Raul went to Denmark the exchange rate was 14 Danish kroner for each £1.

   (a) Raul changed £284.
   Calculate how many Danish kroner he received.

   ....

   ....

   ....

   Answer (a) _____
   (2 marks)

   (b) Raul saw a pair of shoes costing 378 kroner.
   Calculate the price of this in £.

   ....

   ....

   ....

   Answer (b) _____
   (2 marks)

4   Make *y* the subject of this formula.

$$x = \frac{y^2 - 4}{3}$$

....

....

....

....

Answer y = _____
(3 marks)

5 (a) 3 packets of bubble gum and a carton of orange juice cost 65p.
        A packet of bubble gum and 2 cartons of orange juice cost 70p.

   (i) Use x as the price of a packet of bubble gum.
        Use y as the price of a carton of orange juice.
        Write down two equations to represent the information given above.

        Answer (a) (i) _____

        _____
        (2 marks)

   (ii) Solve your equations to find the price of one carton of orange juice.

        Answer (a) (ii) _____ p
        (3 marks)

(b) Jenny bought a large multipack of bubble gum for her family.
    She told her children that if they had 5 packets between them each week, the multipack would last 8 weeks.

   (i) How many weeks should the multipack last if the children have 8 packets of bubble gum between them per week?

        Answer (b) (i) _____ weeks
        (1 mark)

   If the children eat p packets of bubble gum between them per week, the multipack will last n weeks.

   (ii) Write down a formula connecting p and n.

        Answer (b) (ii) _____
        (3 marks)

6 A mountaineer recorded the temperature as he climbed a mountain. His results are below.

Height in feet	2700	3300	4100	5800	6300	7400	8200
Temperature in degrees Celsius	8.5	5	2.5	−3.5	−6	−8	−11.5

(a) Display the information as a scatter diagram using the following grid.

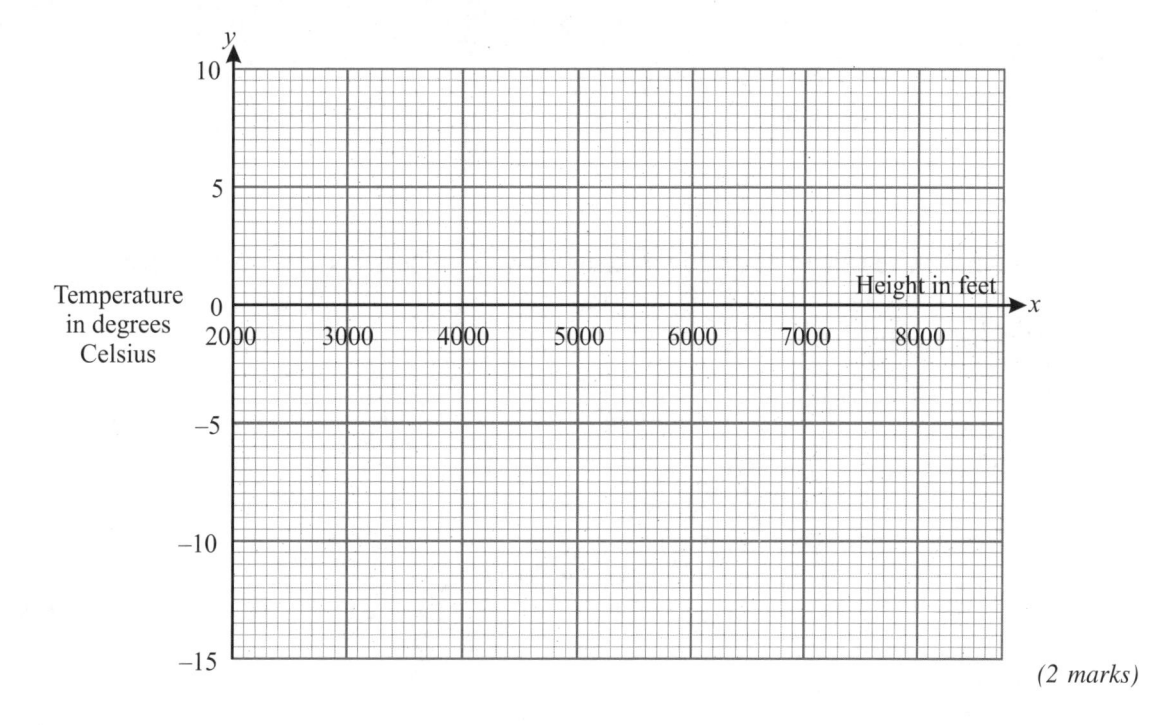

(2 marks)

(b) Describe the correlation in your scatter diagram.

Answer (b) _____

(1 mark)

(c) Draw a line of best fit on your scatter diagram.

(1 mark)

(d) Use your line of best fit to estimate the temperature when he was at a height of 6800 feet.

Answer (d) _____ °C

(1 mark)

7   The rule for getting from one term in a sequence to the next is

'Multiply the previous term by 3, and then add 2'.

(a) Write down the next two terms in the sequence

1,   5,   17,   53, ...

Answer (a) _____ and _____
(2 marks)

(b) Use the above rule to write down the next two numbers in the sequences which start

(i) 0, ...

Answer (b) (i) _____ and _____
(2 marks)

(ii) –3,   –7, ...

Answer (b) (ii) _____ and _____
(2 marks)

8   Solve the simultaneous equations
$$9x - 4y = 20$$
$$3x - 2y = 7.$$

Answers $x =$ _____

$y =$ _____
(4 marks)

9   As part of a survey, a group of people were asked if they were happier this year than at the same time last year.

$\frac{3}{8}$ said they were much happier,

$\frac{1}{3}$ said they were slightly happier,

$\frac{1}{4}$ said they were slightly less happy,

and the rest said they were much less happy.

(a) Draw an accurate and clearly labelled pie chart to represent this information.
Use the circle below.

....

....

....

(4 marks)

(b) Forty-eight people were asked altogether.
How many people said they were much happier?

....

....

....

....

Answer (b) _____

(2 marks)

10   Show how the shaded shape will tessellate using the grid below.
     You should draw at least 6 shapes.

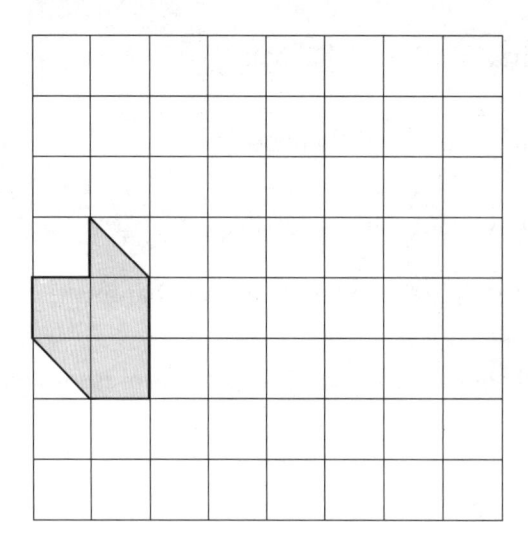

(3 marks)

11   Calculate the following. Give your answers as fractions in their simplest forms.

(a) $\frac{5}{6} - \frac{3}{5}$

....

....

....

Answer (a) _____
(2 marks)

(b) $\frac{2}{7} \times \frac{3}{8}$

....

....

....

Answer (b) _____
(2 marks)

12 (a) Simplify

(i) $x^5 \times x^7$.

Answer (a) (i) _____ (1 mark)

(ii) $\dfrac{6y^7}{2y^2}$.

Answer (a) (ii) _____ (1 mark)

(b) Solve
$4t + 12 < 4$.

Answer (b) _____ (2 marks)

(c) Rearrange the formula below to make u the subject.

$d = \dfrac{u+v}{7}$

Answer (c) _____ (2 marks)

13 (a) The area, A cm², of triangle Y is given by: $A = 2x$.

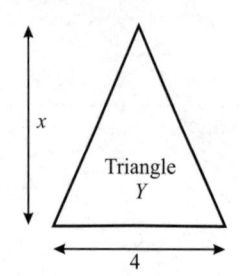

(i) Complete the table by calculating values of A for the given values of x.

x	0	1.5	3
A	0		

(1 mark)

(ii) On the grid opposite, draw a graph of $A = 2x$.

(1 mark)

(b) The area, A cm², of triangle Z is given by: $A = x^2$.

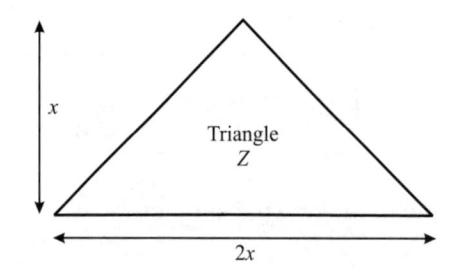

(i) Complete the table by calculating values of A for the given values of x.

x	0	0.5	1	1.5	2	2.5	3
A	0			2.25		6.25	

(2 marks)

(ii) On the grid opposite, draw a graph of $A = x^2$.

(2 marks)

(c) Using your graphs, find the value of x for which the area of triangle Y is the same as the area of triangle Z.

....

....

Answer (c) $x =$ _____

(1 mark)

Leave blank

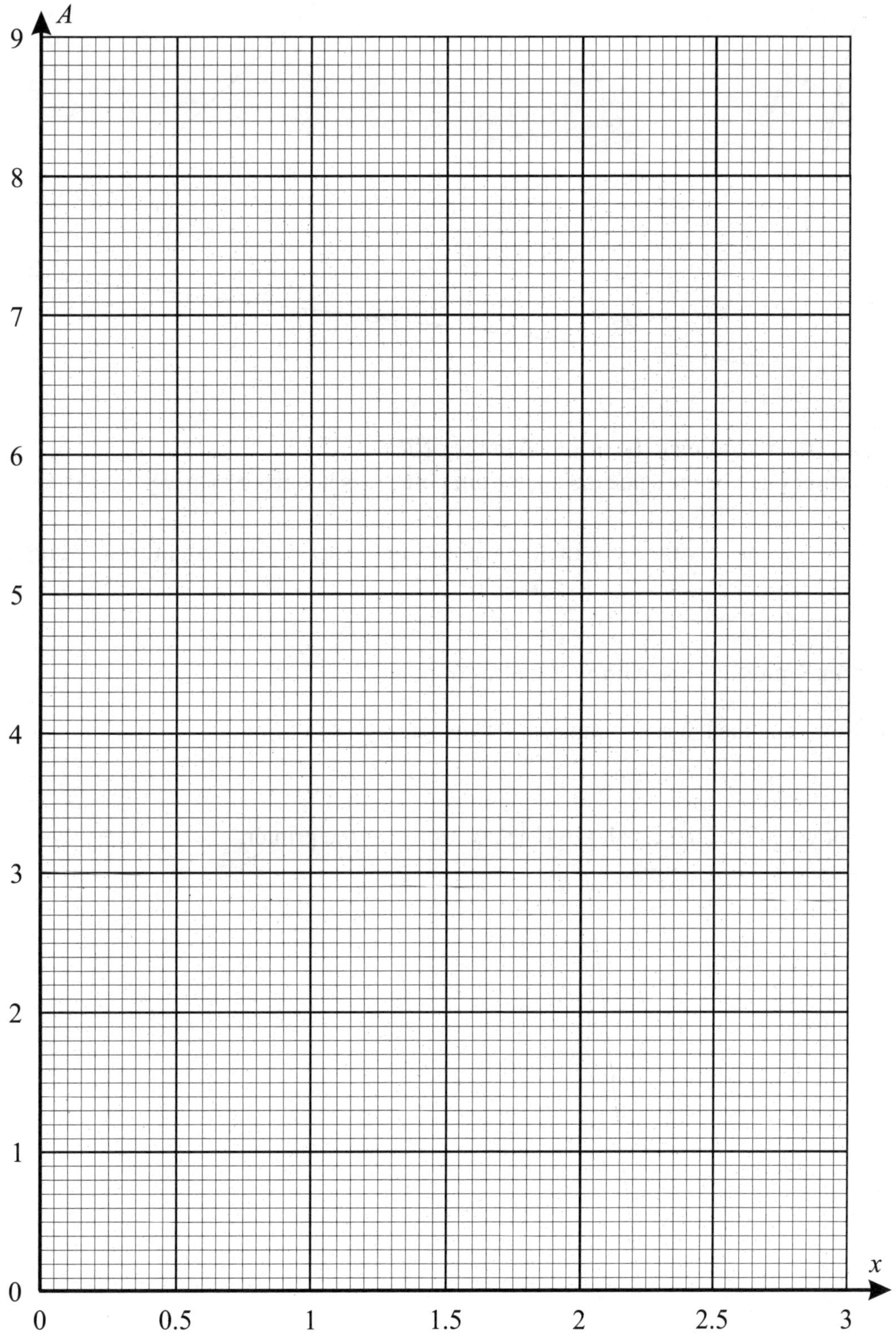

14 The diagram below shows the plan of an office drawn to a scale of 1 cm to 2 metres.

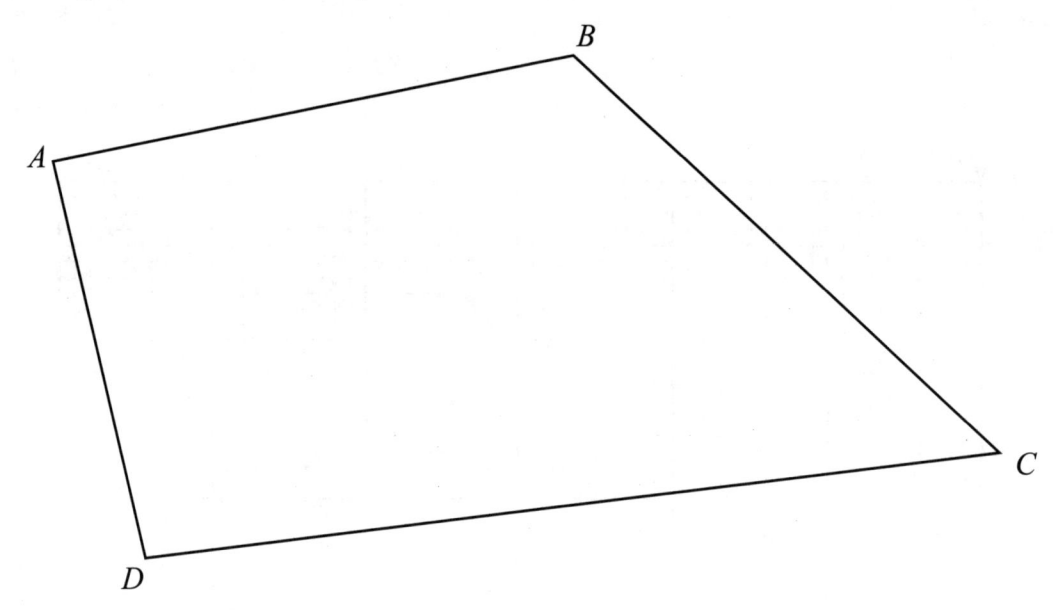

A new printer is going to be installed in the office.
The printer must be the same distance from point *A* as it is from point *D*.

(a) Draw accurately the locus of all the points in the office equidistant from *A* and *D*.

(2 marks)

The printer must also be within 18 metres of point *C*.

(b) Construct the locus of points which are exactly 18 m from *C*.

(2 marks)

(c) Show on the diagram all possible positions for the printer.

(1 mark)

15 In the following diagram, *AB* and *CD* are parallel.
    Angle *BCD* = 38°.
    BCE is a straight line.

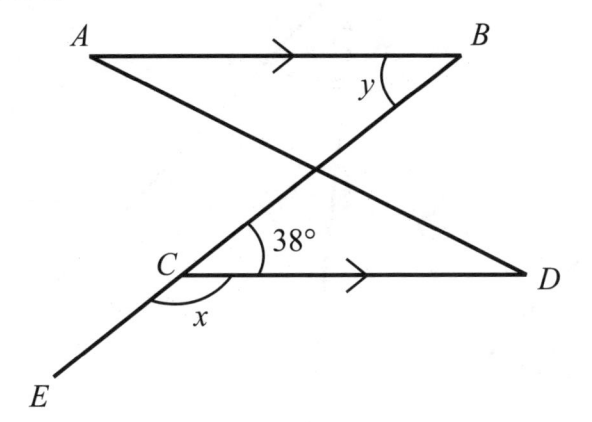

(a) (i) Find the angle marked *x*.

    ....

    Answer (a) (i) x = _____ °

    (ii) Give a reason for your answer.

    Answer (a) (ii) _____

    _____
    (2 marks)

(b) (i) Work out the angle marked *y*.

    ....

    Answer (b) (i) y = _____ °

    (ii) Give a reason for your answer.

    Answer (b) (ii) _____

    _____
    (2 marks)

16 The triangles *ABC* and *XYZ* are similar.

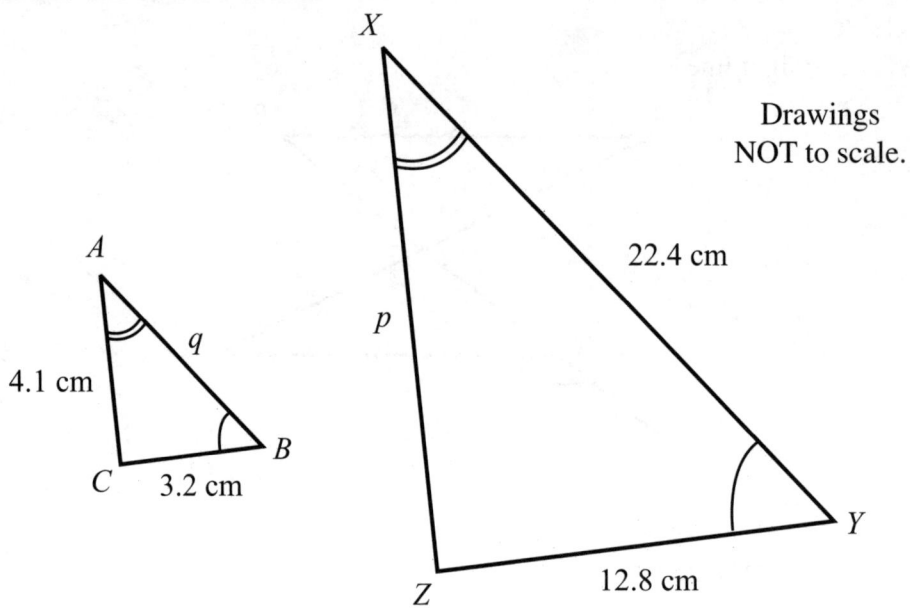

Drawings NOT to scale.

Find the length marked
(a) *p*,

Answer (a) _____ cm

(3 marks)

(b) *q*.

Answer (b) _____ cm

(2 marks)

17 The chairs made by a furniture manufacturer are sometimes slightly damaged during the manufacturing process.
The probability that a chair is damaged is 0.2.

(a) Two chairs are chosen at random.
   (i) Finish this probability tree diagram to show the possible outcomes.

   First chair   **Second chair**

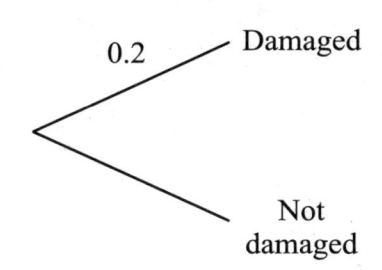

   0.2 ── Damaged

   ── Not damaged

   (2 marks)

   (ii) Calculate the probability that at least 1 of the chairs is not damaged.

   ....
   ....
   ....
   ....

   Answer (a) (ii) _____
   (3 marks)

(b) A furniture store buys 50 of these chairs.
   (i) How many of these chairs can they expect to be damaged?

   ....

   Answer (b) (i) _____
   (3 marks)

   (ii) Explain why your answer is only an approximation.

   Answer (b) (ii) _____

   _____

   _____
   (2 marks)

18 The lengths, to the nearest centimetre, of 24 worms have been recorded in the table below.

Length of worm, in cm	5	6	7	8	9
Frequency	3	7	5	6	3

(a) (i) Write down the median length of the worms.

....

Answer (a) _____ cm

(1 mark)

(ii) Write down the range of the lengths of the worms.

....

Answer (b) _____ cm

(1 mark)

(iii) The lengths of 7 different worms have a median of 8 cm and a range of 10 cm. One of the worms is 10 cm long. Give a possible list of the lengths of these 7 worms.

....

Answer (c) _____

(2 marks)

(b) The weights of the original 24 worms are recorded in a cumulative table.

Weight of worm, in g	2.0	2.2	2.4	2.6	2.8	3.0
Cumulative frequency	0	2	5	13	20	24

(i) On the axes below, draw a cumulative frequency graph to represent this information.

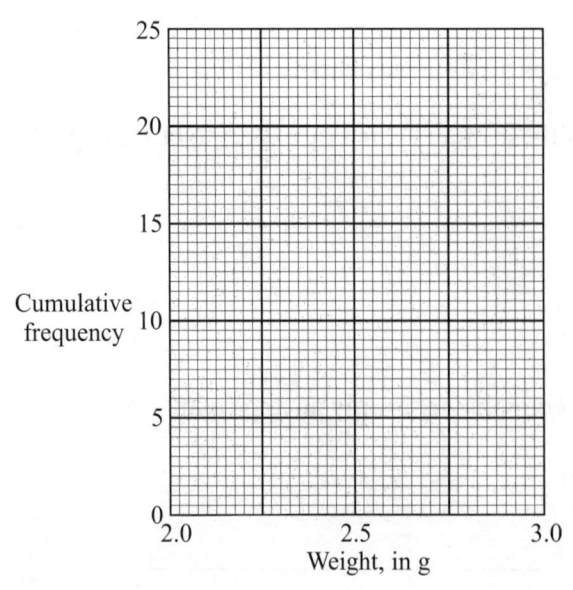

(3 marks)

(ii) Use the cumulative frequency graph to estimate the median weight of the worms.

Answer (b) (ii) _____ g

(2 marks)

General Certificate of Secondary Education

GCSE
Mathematics
Paper 2A – calculator paper

Intermediate Tier

Time allowed: 2 hours.

Centre name	
Centre number	
Candidate number	

Surname	
Other names	
Candidate signature	

In addition to this paper you may need:
- A ruler.
- A protractor.
- A pair of compasses.
- An electronic calculator.
- Tracing paper may be used.

Instructions to candidates
- Write your name and other details in the spaces provided above.
- Answer **all** questions in the spaces provided.
- Do all rough work on the paper.
- Take the value of π to be 3.142, or use the π button on your calculator.

Information for candidates
- The marks available are given in brackets at the end of each question or part-question.
- You may get marks for method, even if your answer is incorrect.
- In calculations show clearly how you work out your answers.
- You are expected to use a calculator where appropriate.
- There are 20 questions in this paper. There are no blank pages.

Advice to candidates
- Work steadily through the paper.
- Don't spend too long on one question.
- If you have time at the end, go back and check your answers.

© 2001 CGP

1   Work out

   (a) 9 squared,

   ....

   Answer (a) _____
   (1 mark)

   (b) 7 cubed,

   ....

   Answer (b) _____
   (1 mark)

   (c) 3^4,

   ....

   Answer (c) _____
   (1 mark)

   (d) 4×10^3,

   ....

   Answer (d) _____
   (1 mark)

   (e) 2.6×10^2.

   ....

   Answer (e) _____
   (1 mark)

2   The pie chart below shows the reasons given by 30 CGP employees for arriving late to work.

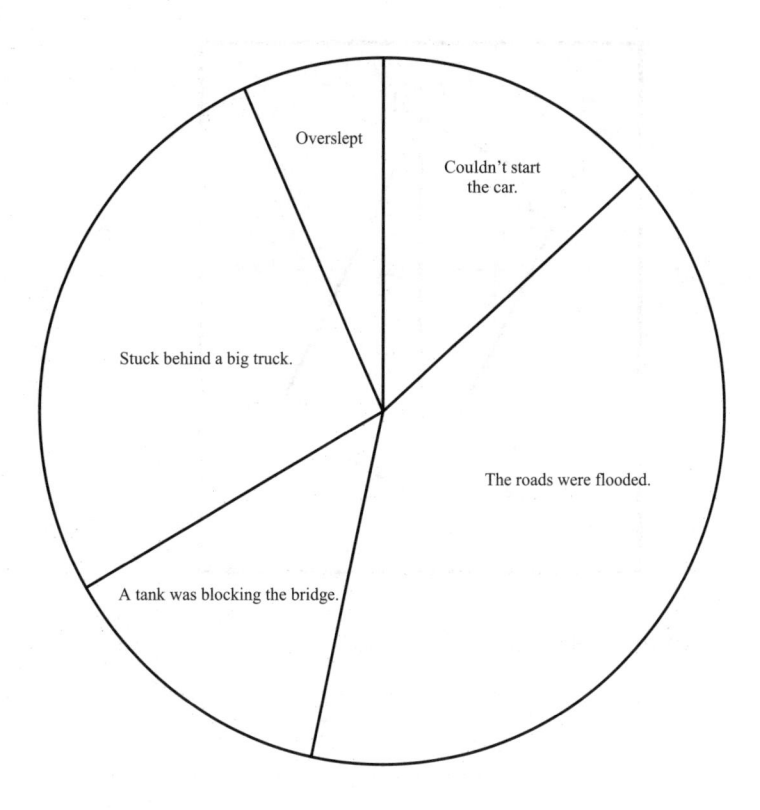

(a) Which is the modal reason for lateness?

Answer (a) _____
(1 mark)

(b) Use the pie chart to work out how many of these employees said they'd been held up by a tank.

....

....

....

....

....

Answer (b) _____
(3 marks)

3   Two right-angled triangles are put together on a 1 cm grid to make a rectangle.

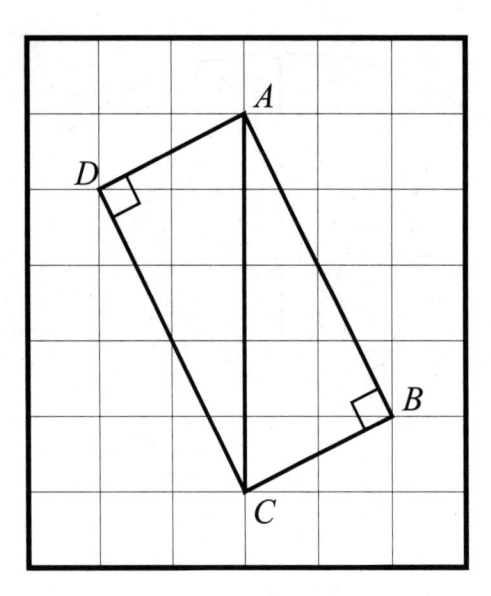

(a) What is the area of the rectangle?
    Remember to state the units.

    ....

    Answer (a) _____
    (2 marks)

(b) Draw a sketch to show how the two triangles can be put together to make an isosceles triangle.

    (2 marks)

4   Calculate the value of

$$\frac{19.8 \times 48.3}{23.46 - 5.17}$$

Give your answer correct to 3 significant figures.

    Answer _____
    (3 marks)

5 One year, when Andy went on holiday to Greece, the exchange rate was

£1 = 600 drachmas.

(a) Use the graph below to find out how many drachmas Andy got for £4.75.

Answer (a) _____

(2 marks)

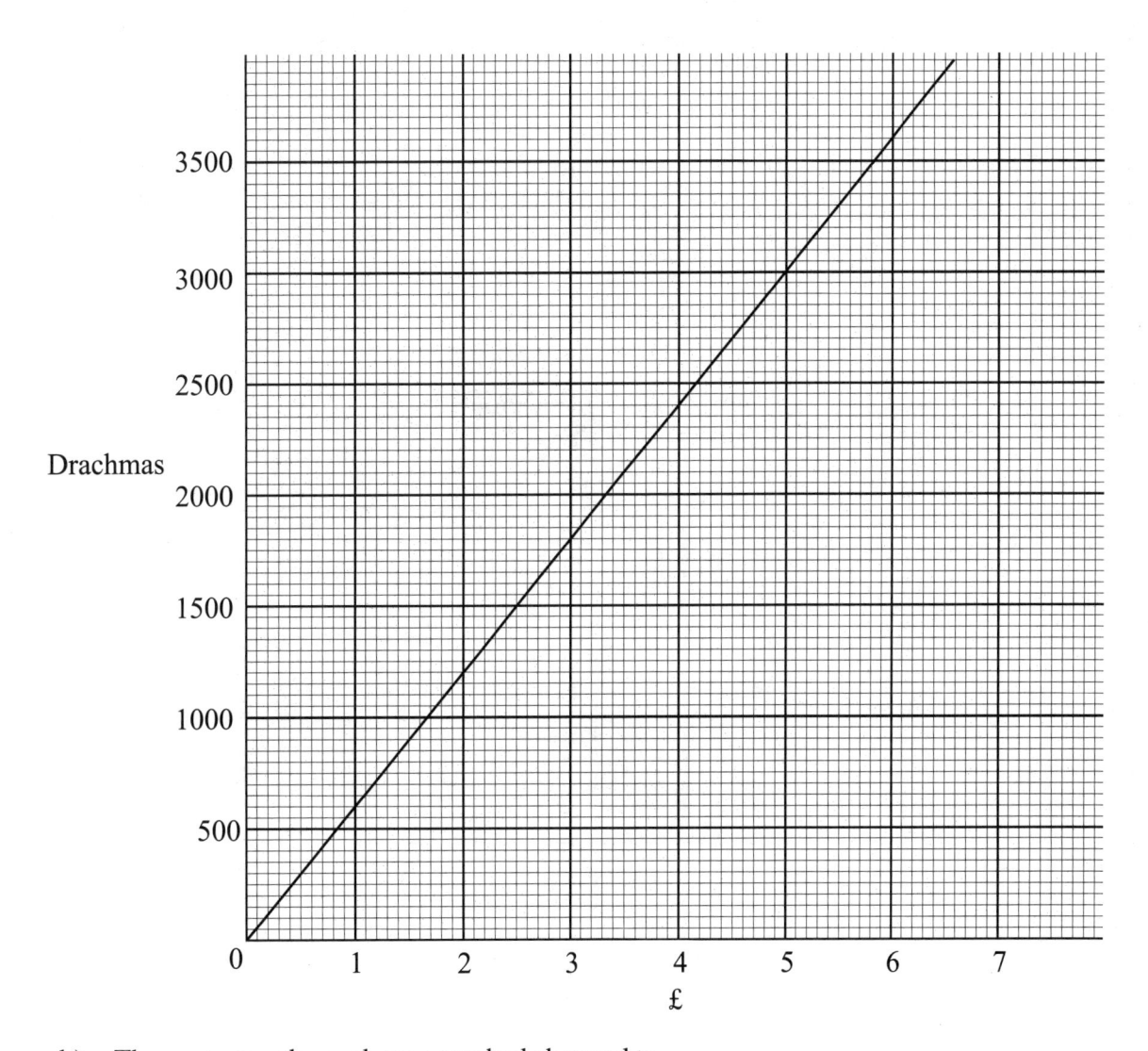

b) The next year, the exchange rate had changed to

£1 = 420 drachmas.

Draw a line on the grid above that could be used to convert money at this new rate.

(3 marks)

6 (a) Reflect the 'T' shape in the y-axis.

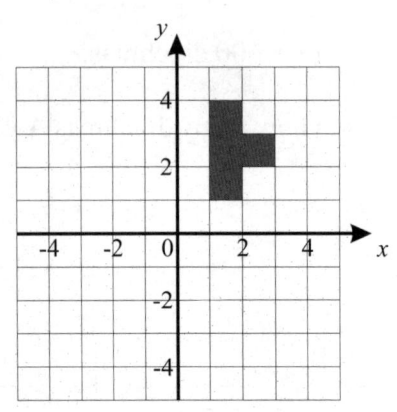

(2 marks)

(b) Rotate the 'T' shape 90° clockwise, centre (0,0).

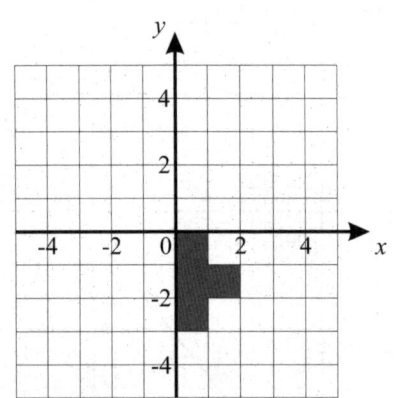

(2 marks)

(c) Translate the 'T' shape 3 units to the right, and 4 units down.

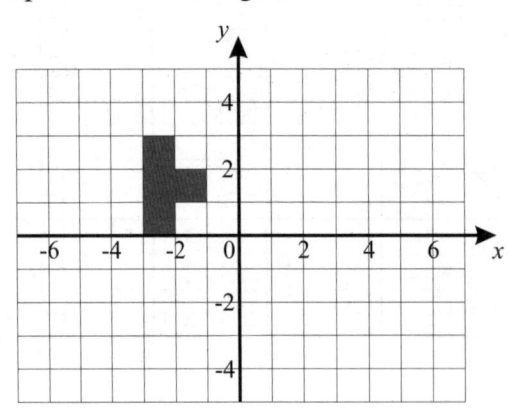

(1 mark)

7 A pair of socks costs n pounds.
A pair of shoes costs $9(n + 2)$ pounds.

(a) Write an expression, in terms of n, for the cost of 6 pairs of socks.

Answer (a) _____

(1 mark)

(b) Write an expression, in terms of *n*, for the cost of 6 pairs of shoes.

*Answer (b)*_____
(1 mark)

(c) George buys 6 pairs of socks and 6 pairs of shoes.
He pays £228.

   (i) Form an equation in *n*.

....

*Answer (c)(i)*_____
(2 marks)

   (ii) Solve your equation to find the cost of a pair of socks.

....

....

....

*Answer (c)(ii)*_____
(2 marks)

8 (a) Expand $x^2(7x^2 - 2x + 3)$

....

....

*Answer (a)*_____
(2 marks)

(b) Expand and simplify $(6x + 3)(2x - 4)$

....

....

....

*Answer (b)*_____
(3 marks)

9

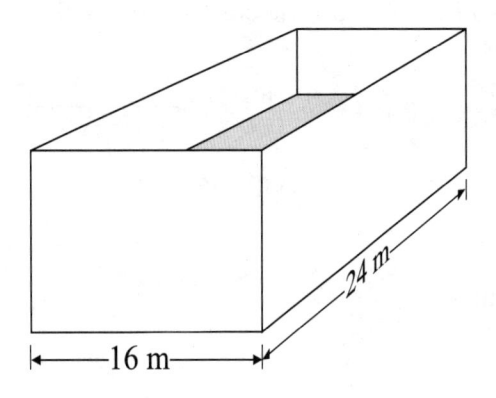

Water is stored in a tank which is cuboid in shape and which has a rectangular base. The sides of the base are 24 m and 16 m long. The water is 3.5 m deep.

(a) Work out the volume of the water.

....

....

Answer (a)_____m³

(2 marks)

More water is put in the tank. The depth of the water rises to 5.4 m.

(b) Calculate the percentage increase in the volume of the water in the tank.
Give your answer to 3 significant figures.

....

....

Answer (b)_____%

(3 marks)

10 (a) Before the last World Bean Flicking Competition, Albert had a personal best of 3.80 m. During the championship, his personal best improved to 106% of its previous value.
Calculate his new personal best.
Give your answer to an appropriate degree of accuracy.

....

....

....

Answer (a)_____m

(3 marks)

(b) At the same championships, the world record for bean flicking increased from 4.24 metres to 4.81 metres.
Calculate the percentage increase.

....

....

....

*Answer (b)*_____%
(3 marks)

11

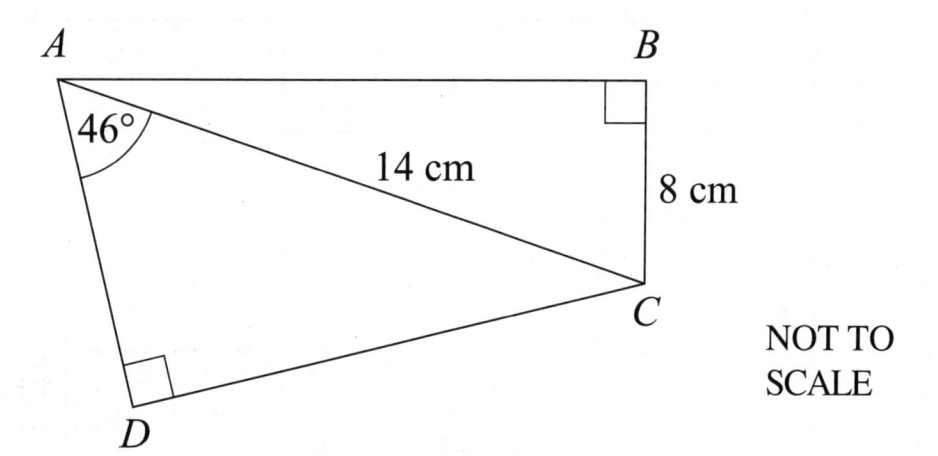

A ... *B*
46°
14 cm
8 cm
C
D

NOT TO SCALE

(a) Calculate angle *BAC*.

....

....

*Answer (a)*_____°
(3 marks)

(b) Calculate the length of *AD*.

....

....

*Answer (b)*_____cm
(3 marks)

12 Minjita travelled from home to her grandmother's house. She cycled to the train station, and then took a train to her grandmother's station where she hailed a taxi for the remaining journey.

(a) Use the information below to construct a travel graph showing Minjita's journey.
Minjita left home at 0900.
At 14.4 km/h, it took her 5 minutes to cycle to the train station.
She waited 14 minutes before the train left.
The train travelled for a further 11 km at a speed of 66 km/h.
It then took her 6 minutes at a steady speed of 38 km/h by taxi to get to her grandmother's.

....

....

(4 marks)

(b) How far has Minjita travelled by 0925?

Answer (b)_____km

(1 mark)

13   When Jack finds something, it is either a beetle, a worm, or a slug.
      The probability that it is a slug is 0.2.
      The probability that it is a beetle is 0.1.

      (i) What is the probability that Jack's find is a worm?

      ....

      ....

      Answer (i) _____
      (2 marks)

      (ii) If Jack finds 20 grubs, how many beetles would he expect to have?

      ....

      ....

      Answer (ii) _____
      (2 marks)

14

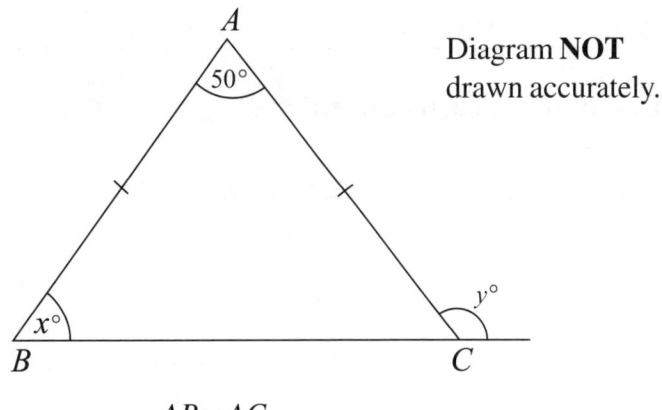

Diagram **NOT** drawn accurately.

AB = AC

Work out the sizes of the angles marked

(a) x,

Answer (a) x = _____

(b) y.

Answer (b) y = _____
(3 marks)

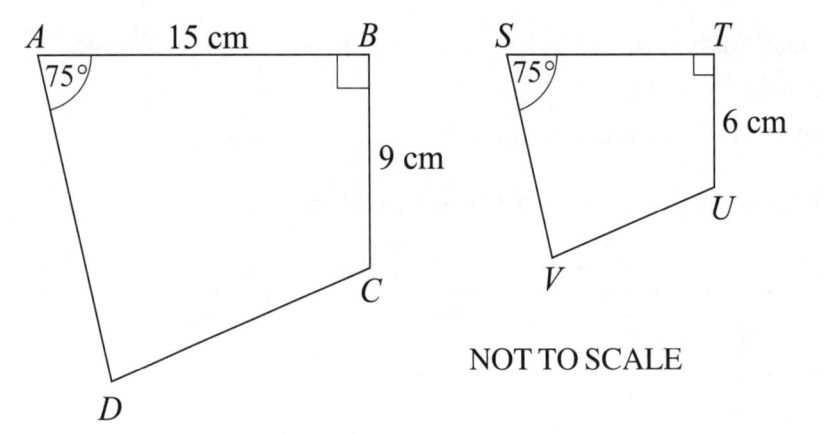

15. Quadrilateral ABCD is similar to quadrilateral STUV.

Calculate the length of the side ST.

Answer _____ cm
(2 marks)

16. (a) 7 employees arrive at work at the following times.

Employee	P	Q	R	S	T	U	V
Time of arrival (am)	8:31	8:26	8:39	8:33	8:30	8:29	8:36

(i) What is their median time of arrival?

Answer (a)(i) _____
(1 mark)

(ii) Employees who arrive after 8:30 am are late.
Calculate the mean number of minutes late of the 4 latecomers.

Answer (a)(ii) _____ mins
(3 marks)

(b) The working day finishes at 5.00 pm. The same 7 employees leave work at the following times.

Employee	P	Q	R	S	T	U	V
Time of departure (pm)	5:03	5:13	5:01	5:07	5:11	5:04	5:14

(i) Plot their time of leaving against their time of arrival on the scatter diagram below. The times for P, Q and R have been plotted for you.

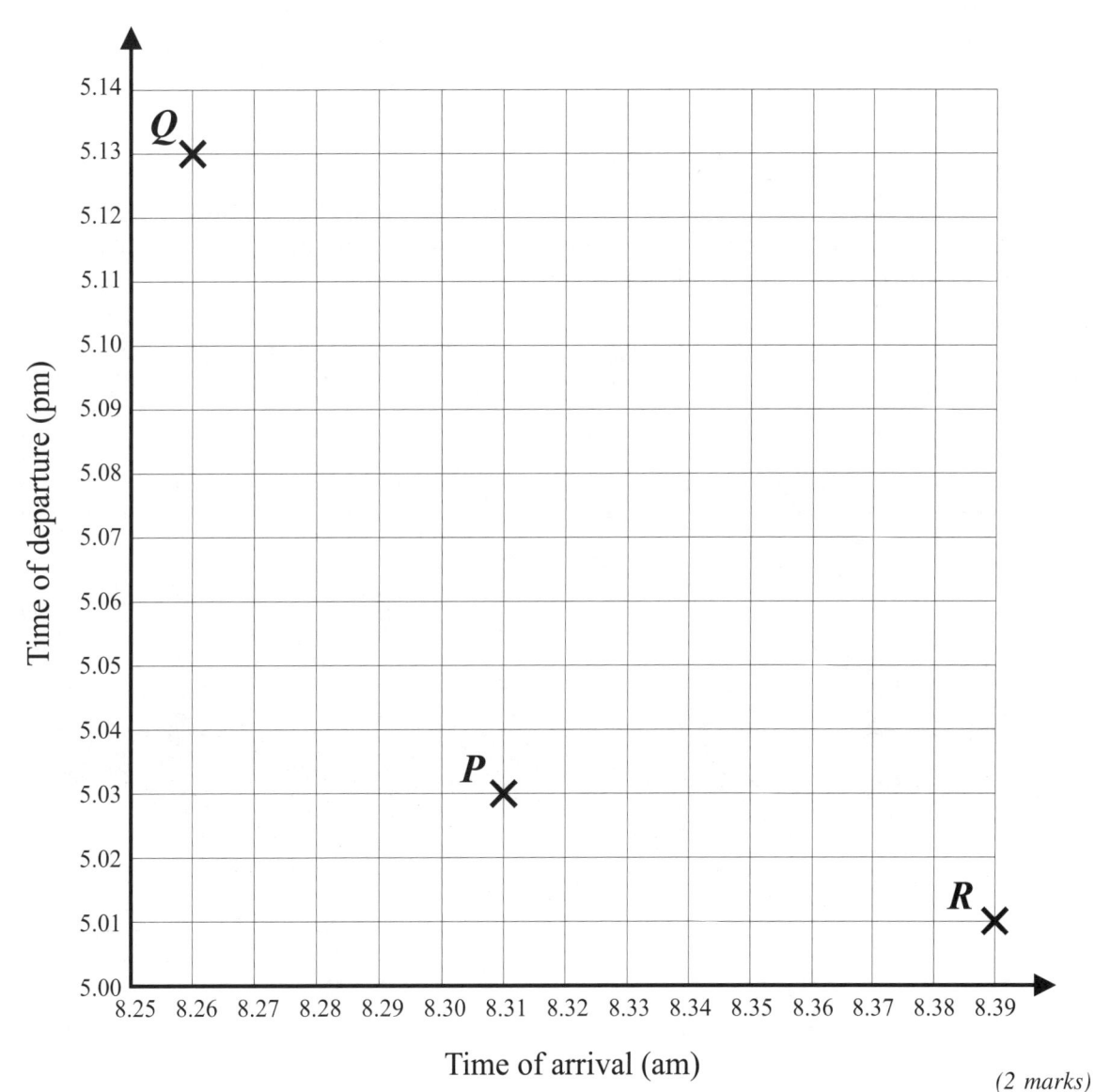

(2 marks)

(ii) What conclusion can you draw from this scatter diagram?

Answer (b)(ii) _____

_____

(1 mark)

17 A lorry contains 329 boxes of chocolate biscuits.
Each box contains either plain chocolate or milk chocolate biscuits.

The probability that a box selected at random contains plain chocolate biscuits is $\frac{2}{5}$ of the probability that the box holds milk chocolate biscuits.

(a) Calculate the number of boxes containing plain chocolate biscuits.

....

....

*Answer (a)*_____
(3 marks)

Each box contains 28 packets of biscuits.
One in every 12 packets of plain chocolate biscuits contains a prize-winning voucher.
One in every 24 packets of milk chocolate biscuits has a prize-winning voucher in it.
A packet is to be selected at random from the lorry.

(b) Calculate the probability that the packet will contain a prize-winning voucher.

....

....

*Answer (b)*_____
(3 marks)

18 (a) Solve the equations:

  (i) $4x = \frac{1}{8}$

  ....

  *Answer (a)(i)*_____
  (1 mark)

  (ii) $2x^2 - 6x + 4 = 0$

  ....

  ....

  *Answer (a)(ii)*_____
  (2 marks)

(b) Solve the inequality $4(x+8) < x-1$.

....

*Answer (b)*_____
(3 marks)

(c) The graph of $5y = 6x - 10$ is drawn.

(i) On the same axes, draw the graph of $5y = 2x + 20$.

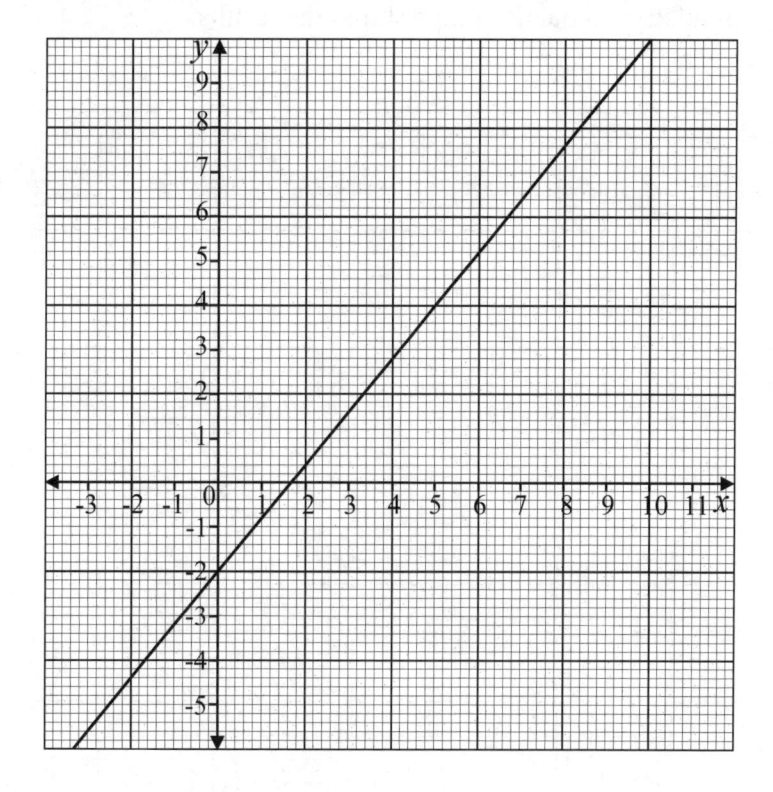

(2 marks)

(ii) Solve the simultaneous equations:

$$5y = 6x - 10$$
$$5y = 2x + 20$$

Answer (c)(ii) x = _____ y = _____

(2 marks)

19 Write down the *n*th term for each of the following sequences.

(a) 2, 4, 6, 8, ...

.... *Answer (a)_____*

(1 mark)

(b) 2, 5, 8, 11, ...

.... *Answer (b)_____*

(1 mark)

(c) 1, 4, 9, 16, ...

.... *Answer (c)_____*

(1 mark)

(d) 3, 12, 27, 48, ...

.... *Answer (d)_____*

(2 marks)

20 The amount of time taken to complete an assault course was recorded for a group of 35 university lecturers.

The following cumulative frequency graph shows the results.

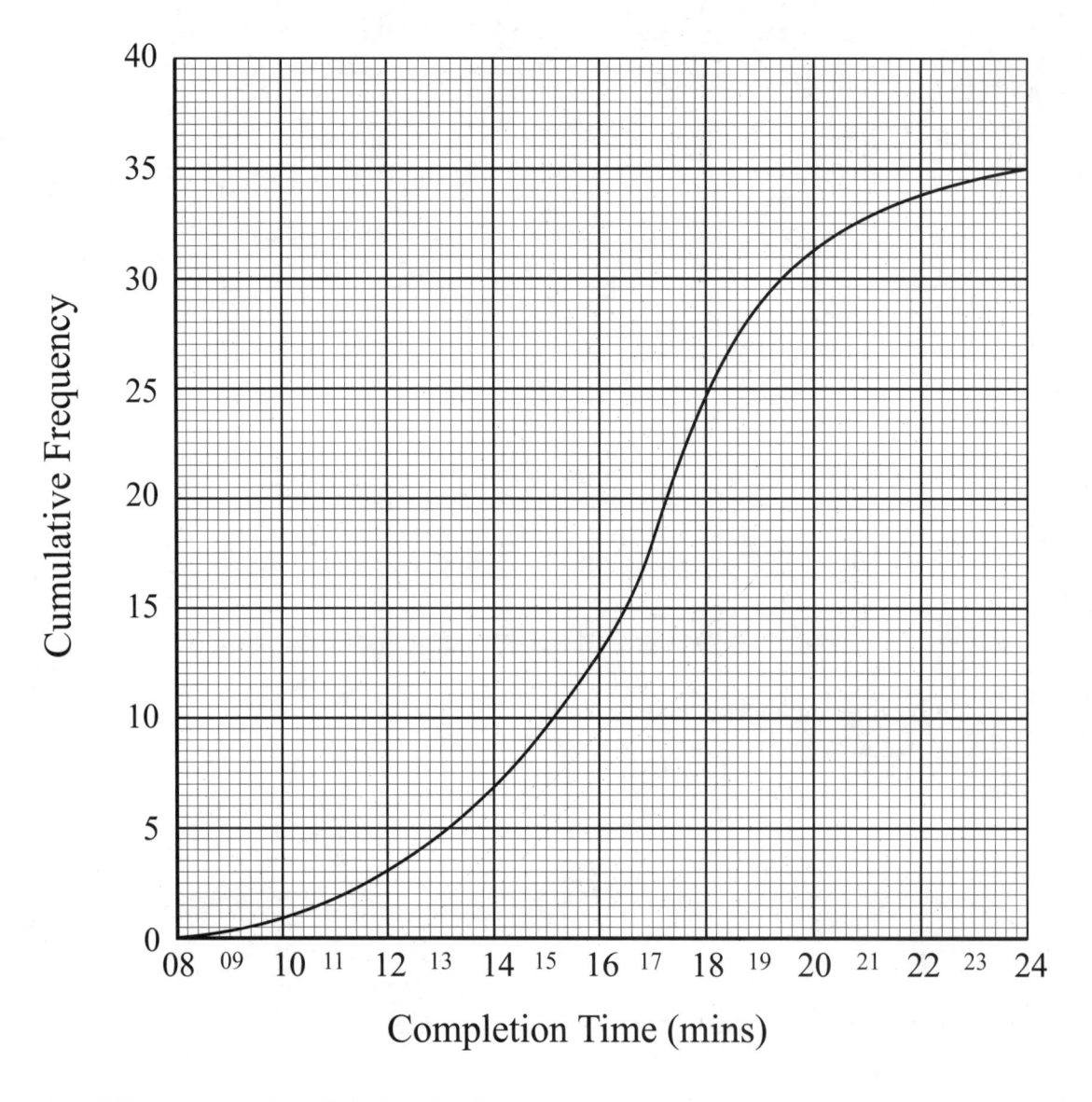

(a) What is the median finishing time?

....

Answer (a) _____ mins
(1 mark)

(b) What is the interquartile range?

....

Answer (b) _____ mins
(3 marks)

General Certificate of Secondary Education

GCSE
Mathematics
Paper 2B – non-calculator paper

Intermediate Tier

Time allowed: 2 hours.

Centre name	
Centre number	
Candidate number	

Surname	
Other names	
Candidate signature	

In addition to this paper you may need:
- A ruler.
- A protractor.
- A pair of compasses.
- Tracing paper may be used.

Instructions to candidates
- Write your name and other details in the spaces provided above.
- Answer **all** questions in the spaces provided.
- Do all rough work on the paper.

Information for candidates
- The marks available are given in brackets at the end of each question or part-question.
- You may get marks for method, even if your answer is incorrect.
- In calculations show clearly how you work out your answers.
- There are 20 questions in this paper. There are no blank pages.

Advice to candidates
- Work steadily through the paper.
- Don't spend too long on one question.
- If you have time at the end, go back and check your answers.

© 2001 CGP

1 (a) (i) Give the next two terms in this number sequence.

192, 96, 48, 24, ... , ...

Answer (a) (i) _____ , _____
(1 mark)

(ii) What is the rule for finding the next term of the sequence?

Answer (a) (ii) _____

_____
(1 mark)

(b) (i) Give the next term in this number sequence.

1, 3, 7, 15, ...

Answer (b) (i) _____
(1 mark)

(ii) What is the rule for finding the next term of this sequence?

Answer (b) (ii) _____

_____
(2 marks)

(c) (i) What is the nth term of the number sequence

$$\frac{1}{2}, \frac{1}{5}, \frac{1}{8}, \frac{1}{11}, \frac{1}{14}, \ldots\ldots ?$$

....

....

Answer (c) (i) _____
(2 marks)

(ii) What is the nth term of the number sequence

$$\frac{3}{5}, \frac{2}{5}, \frac{1}{5}, 0, -\frac{1}{5}, \ldots\ldots ?$$

....

....

Answer (c) (ii) _____
(2 marks)

2
$$a = 8 \times 10^2$$
$$b = 4 \times 10^3$$

(a) Find the value of $a \times b$, giving your answer in standard form.

....

Answer (a) _____
(2 marks)

(b) Find the value of $a + b$, giving your answer as an ordinary number.

....

Answer (b) _____
(2 marks)

3 Charley has 145 CDs to take with him to university. He tries to fit them all into shoe boxes. Each shoe box will hold 34 CDs.

(a) How many shoe boxes will he need to hold all of his CDs?

....

Answer (a) _____
(2 marks)

(b) Each shoe box costs £13 (including shoes). How much will he have to spend on shoes to get the number of shoe boxes required to hold all of his CDs?

....

Answer (b) _____
(2 marks)

(c) He decides to only take completely filled boxes of CDs. How many CDs will he have to leave behind?

....

Answer (c) _____
(2 marks)

Leave blank

4 A bag of sherbet sweets contains four different flavours of sweet: strawberry, orange, blackcurrant and cola. All the sweets are the same size.
The probability of picking a cola sweet at random is 0.2. The probability of picking a strawberry sweet is 0.3. The bag contains the same number of orange and blackcurrant sweets.

(a) What is the probability of picking an orange sweet?

....

....

Answer (a) _____
(2 marks)

Each bag contains 80 sweets.

(b) How many sweets are strawberry flavoured?

....

....

Answer (b) _____
(2 marks)

5 Solve the following equations
(a) $2x - 5 = 45$

....

....

Answer (a) _____
(2 marks)

(b) $2x + 3 = 51 - 4x$

....

....

Answer (b) _____
(2 marks)

6   (a)   Draw in one plane of symmetry on the prism shown.

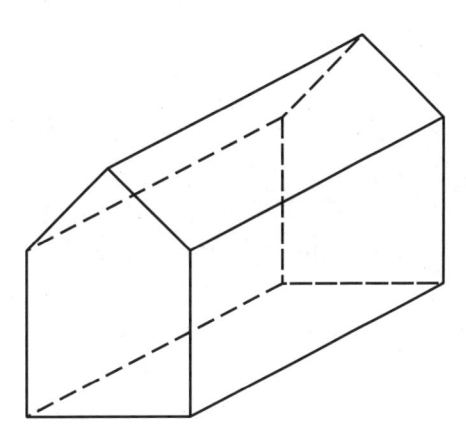

(2 marks)

(b)   Find the angle $x°$ in the shape shown below.

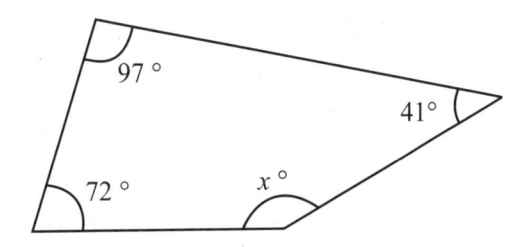

Diagram **NOT** drawn accurately

....

Answer (b) _____

(2 marks)

(c)   The diagram shows a regular pentagon. Find the angle $y°$.

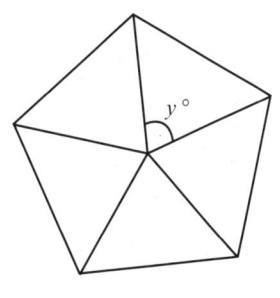

Diagram **NOT** drawn accurately

....

Answer (c) _____

(2 marks)

7   Look at the pattern below.

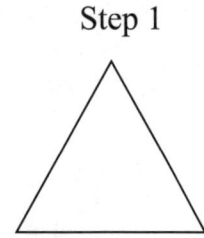

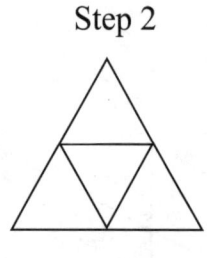

Step 1   Step 2   Step 3

Complete the table below by giving the number of triangles in the pattern at Step *n*.

Step	Number of triangles
1	1
2	4
3	16
n	

(2 marks)

8   There are three paths connecting Penny Bridge to Greenodd. Every day at 9:00am, Dominic walks from Greenodd to Penny Bridge. Every day at the same time, Lisa walks the other way from Penny Bridge to Greenodd.

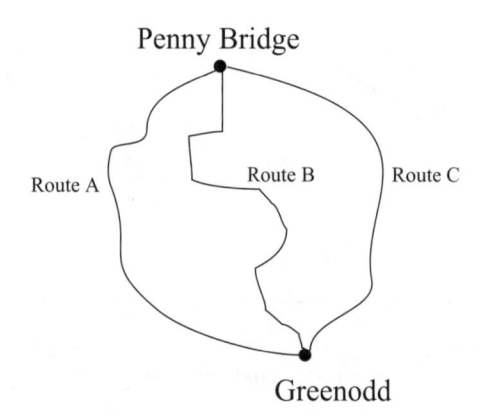

Penny Bridge

Route A   Route B   Route C

Greenodd

The probabilities of Lisa taking routes A and B on any particular day are 0.3 and 0.1 respectively.

(a) What is the probability that Lisa will take route C on any particular day?

Answer (a) _____

(1 mark)

(b) Dominic takes route A on Monday.
What is the probability that he will <u>not</u> pass Lisa on his walk?

....

Answer (b) _____

(2 marks)

(c) Dominic takes route B on Tuesday and route C on Wednesday.
What is the probability that he will meet Lisa on Tuesday and Wednesday?

....

Answer (c) _____
(2 marks)

9 (a) Solve these simultaneous equations

$$4x + 5y = 23$$
$$7y - 2x = 17$$

Answer $x =$ _____
$y =$ _____
(4 marks)

(b) Solve the inequality
$$-6z - 5 < -2z + 19$$

Answer $z >$ _____
(2 marks)

10 Below is a graph produced from a physics experiment.

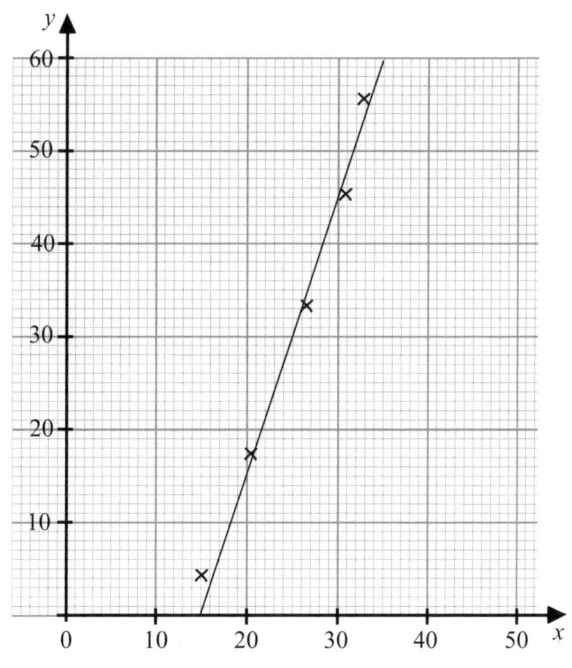

Find the equation of the line.

....

....

Answer _____
(4 marks)

11   Look at the flow diagram below.

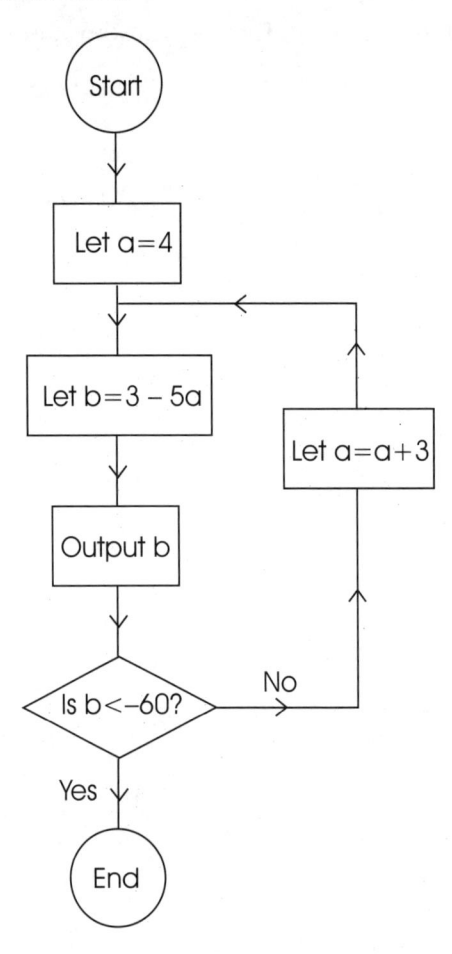

Write down the numbers that will be output.

....

....

....

Answer −17, −32, −47, −62

(6 marks)

12 Four scatter graphs are shown below.

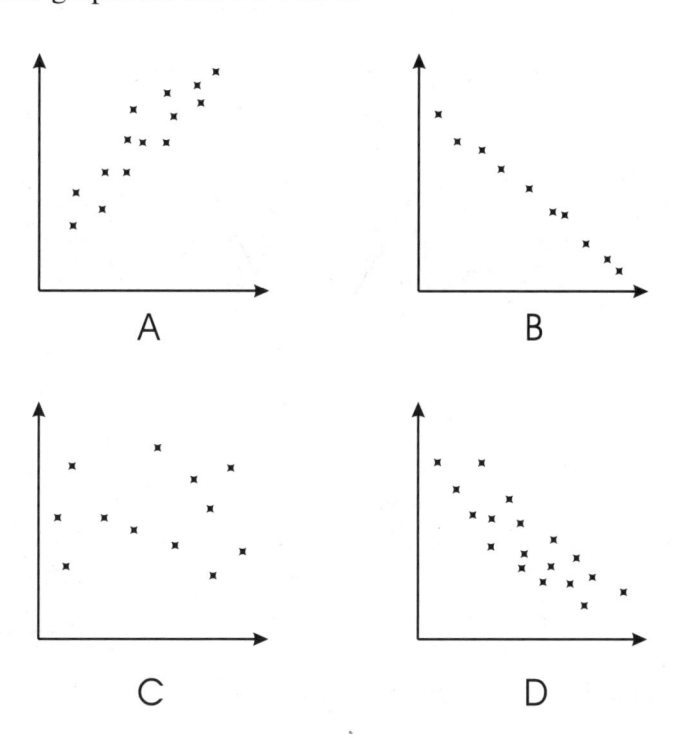

[Scatter graph A: positive correlation]
[Scatter graph B: strong negative correlation]
[Scatter graph C: no correlation]
[Scatter graph D: negative correlation]

Which of the graphs A to D shows

(a) the strongest correlation?

Answer (a) _____
(1 mark)

(b) a positive correlation?

Answer (b) _____
(1 mark)

Which of the graphs A to D is most likely to be showing

(c) results in a maths test and height of candidates?

Answer (c) _____
(1 mark)

(d) age of computers and their selling prices?

Answer (d) _____
(1 mark)

13 The diagram below is not drawn to scale.

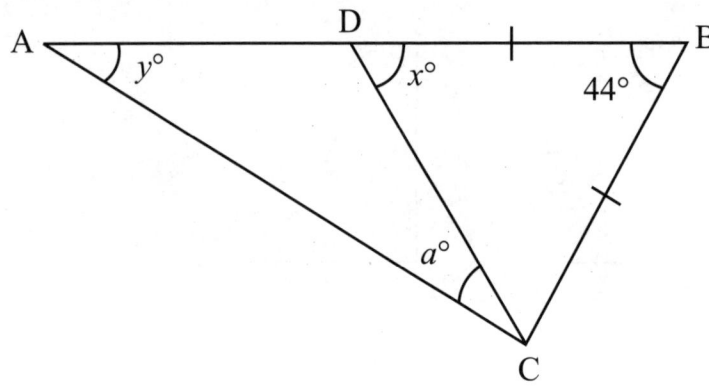

(a) Find the size of the angle marked *x*.

....

Answer (a) _____
(2 marks)

(b) What is the angle *y*, written in terms of *a*?

....

Answer (b) _____
(2 marks)

(c) Find the value of *a* for which AD = DC.

....

....

Answer (c) _____
(2 marks)

14 Andrew dreamt that 50 litres of petrol cost £2.
(a) How much would Andrew pay for 20 litres of petrol in his dream?

....

Answer (a) _____
(2 marks)

Next morning, Andrew drove to the petrol station and paid £17 for 20 litres of petrol.
(b) What was the cost of the petrol per litre in real life?

....

Answer (b) _____
(2 marks)

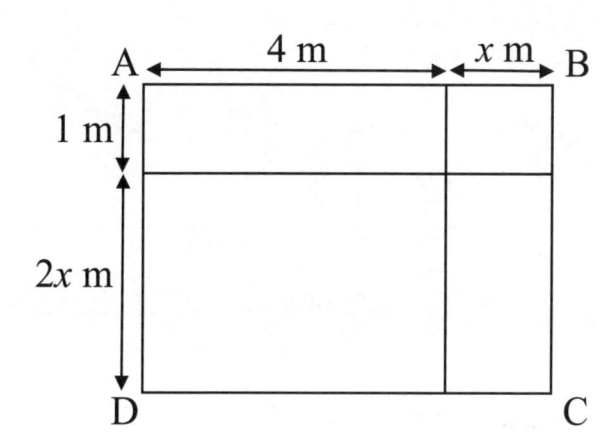

15.

(a) Write down an expression for the
   (i) perimeter of rectangle ABCD,

   ....

   Answer (a)(i) _____
   (1 mark)

   (ii) area of rectangle ABCD.

   ....

   Answer (a)(ii) _____
   (1 mark)

(b) Given that the area of ABCD is actually 15 m², show that $2x^2 + 9x - 11 = 0$.

   _____

   _____

   _____
   (3 marks)

16    $a = 3, b = 2, c = -8$

(a) Calculate the value of $b^2 - 4ac$.

....

Answer (a) _____
(2 marks)

(b) Use your answer to (a) to calculate the two values of the expression

$$\frac{-b \pm \sqrt{b^2 - 4ac}}{2a}$$

....

Answer (b) _____
(3 marks)

17 The table below records the scores of 160 people in a magazine survey called "Are you a fashion victim?". Each person who completes the survey gets a score out of 100.

Score out of 100 marks	Number of people	Cumulative Frequency
$x \leq 10$	2	
$10 < x \leq 20$	3	
$20 < x \leq 30$	6	
$30 < x \leq 40$	8	
$40 < x \leq 50$	15	
$50 < x \leq 60$	34	
$60 < x \leq 70$	49	
$70 < x \leq 80$	33	
$80 < x \leq 90$	8	
$90 < x \leq 100$	2	

a) Complete the third column to show the cumulative frequency of the data.
(2 marks)

b) Draw a cumulative frequency diagram of the data on the graph on the next page.
(3 marks)

Leave blank

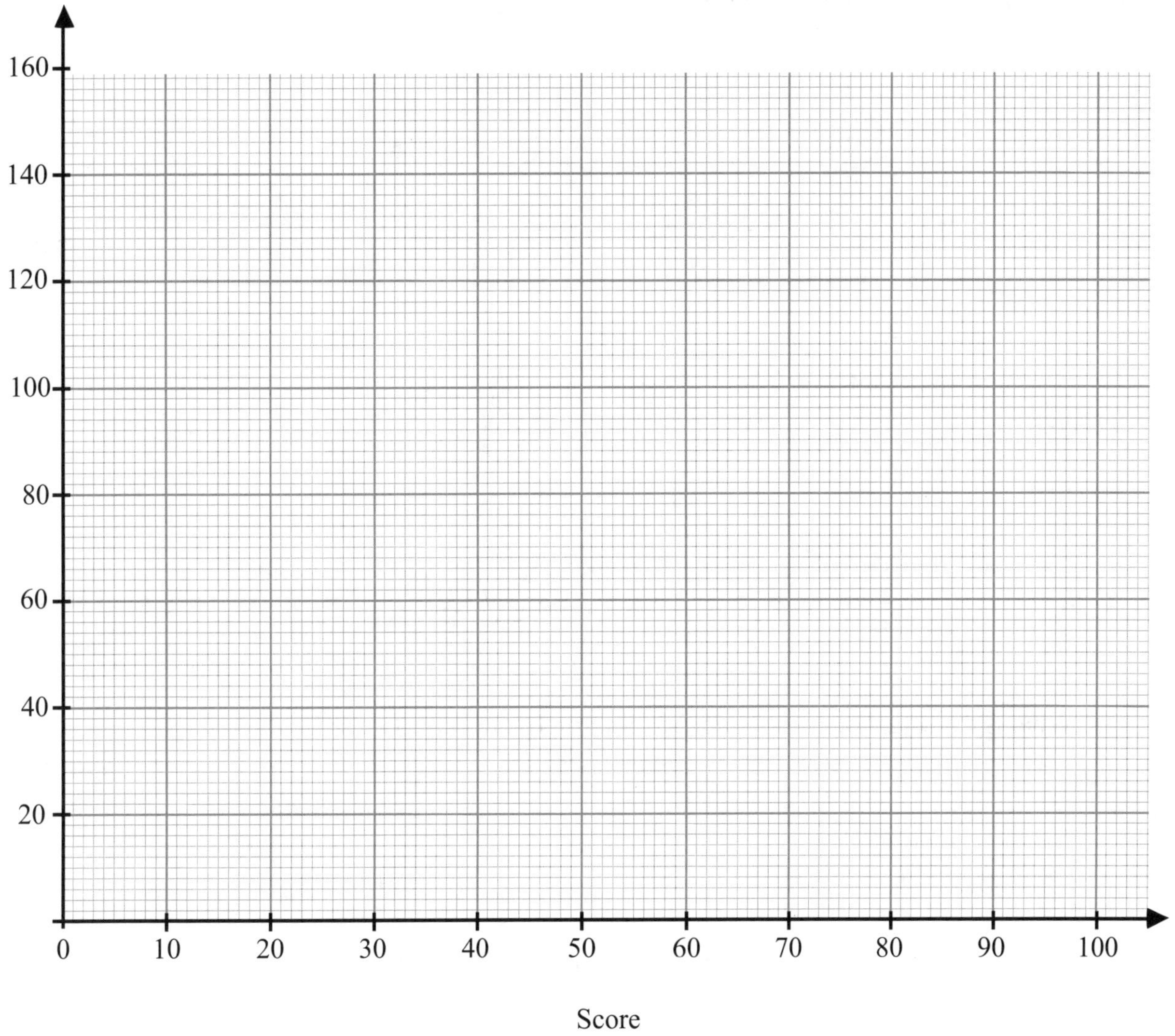

(c) Use the diagram to estimate the median score.

Answer (c) ____________

(1 mark)

(d) Use the diagram to estimate the number of people who scored less than 75.

Answer (d) ____________

(1 mark)

18 The map below has a scale of 1cm to 5 km.

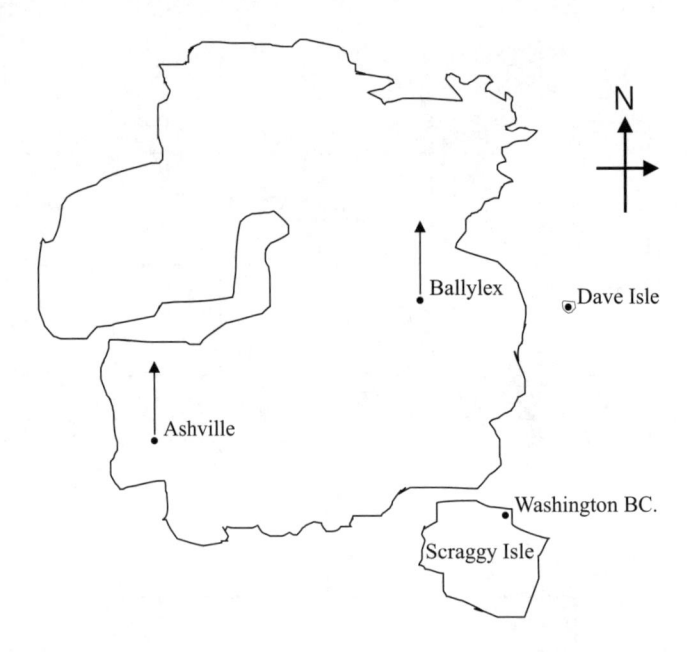

(a) What is the actual distance from Washington BC to Dave Isle?

....

Answer (a) _____

(3 marks)

(b) What is the three figure bearing of Ashville from Ballylex?

....

Answer (b) _____

(2 marks)

19 Below are two identical drawings of a squared-based pyramid, which has four planes of symmetry. Show two of these planes of symmetry by drawing one on each diagram.

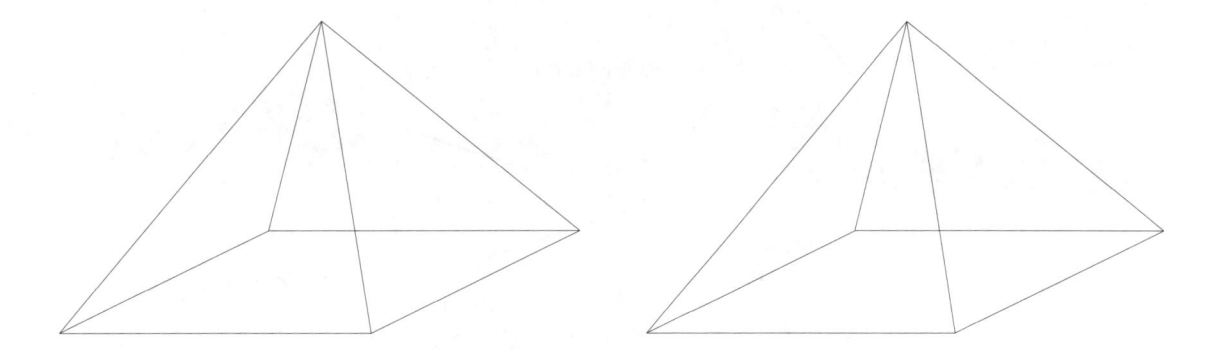

square-based pyramid

(4 marks)

Turn over for next question.

20   250 teenagers were asked to choose their favourite male recording artist from a shortlist of 4. The results are shown in the pie chart below.

Ricky Martin 30%
Ronan Keating 10%
Cliff Richard 44%
Robbie Williams ....%

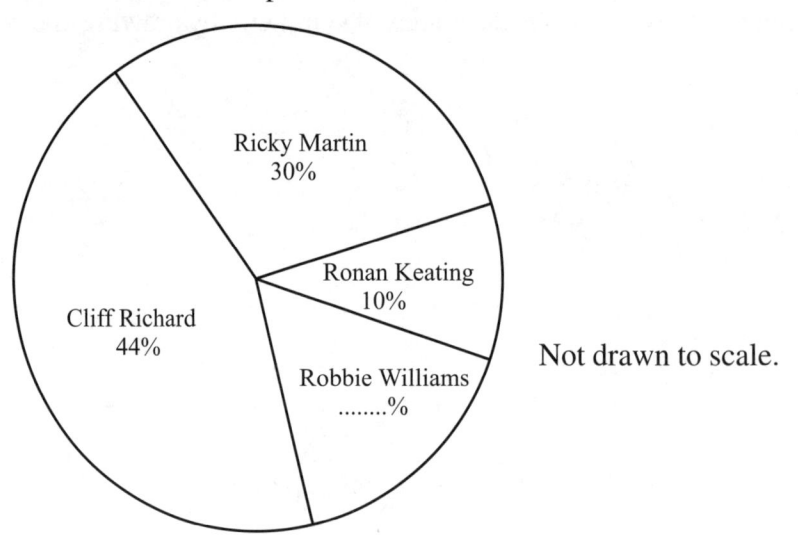

Not drawn to scale.

(a) What percentage of them chose Robbie Williams?

....

Answer (a) _____
(1 mark)

(b) How many people chose Ricky Martin?

....

Answer (b) _____
(1 mark)

(c) Calculate the angle of the sector representing Robbie Williams.

....

Answer (c) _____
(2 marks)

Answers

Paper 1A

1 (a)

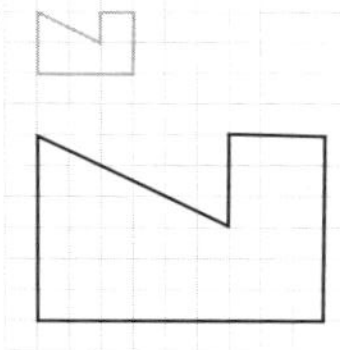

[diagram of net]

2 marks. 1 mark for at least 3 sides correct.

(b) Volume of cuboid = length × width × height
= 12.2 × 3.1 × 5.7 = **215.6 cm³**
2 marks available — 1 mark for the right method, 1 mark for the right answer. (The measurements are given to 1 d.p., so you should give the answer to 1 d.p. But they're not too fussy — so 216, 215.57, 215.574 are also OK.)
Pretty easy — plain, straightforward TRANSFORMATIONS and VOLUMES.

2 $\frac{1.729}{8.1} \times 0.72 = 0.1537 =$ **0.2** to 1 d.p.
3 marks available for correct answer to correct accuracy. 2 marks available if you get the right answer, but write it down with two or three decimal places. 1 mark available if you round down too early and get 0.1 instead of 0.2.
The question's easy — it's the ROUNDING that might be a little tricky.

3 Area of triangle = ½ × base × height = ½ × 2.1 × 1.3 = **1.4 m²**
2 marks available — 1 for right method, 1 for right answer. (The measurements are given to 1d.p., so you should give your answer to 1d.p. But they'll let you get away with 1.37 or 1.365 without losing marks.)

4 2.1 kg apples cost 2.1 × £1.14 = £2.39; 700 g carrots cost 0.7 × £0.78 = £0.55; 3 pumpkins cost 3 × £1.70 = £5.10. Altogether, these cost £2.39 + £0.55 + £5.10 = £8.04. So if Rhonda uses a £20 note, her change will be £20.00 − £8.04 = **£11.96**.
4 marks available — 1 for using the correct methods to find at least two individual item costs, 1 mark for getting at least two of these correct, 1 for the right total cost, and 1 for the correct final answer.
If you messed that up, you'd better get some more practice.

(b) 1 litre (= 1000 ml) of Juicy Juice costs 98p, so 1 ml costs 98p ÷ 1000 = 0.098p. 750 ml of Fresh 'n' Juicy costs 81p, so 1 ml costs 81p ÷ 750 = 0.108p. So *Juicy Juice* is better value for money. (Or you could find the amount per penny, rather than the price per ml — either way is OK.)
3 marks available — 2 for the correct method, 1 for the right answer.

(c) Either work out 14% of £36.99 (= 0.14 × £36.99 = £5.18) and subtract this from the original price, giving £36.99 − £5.18 = **£31.81**.
Or take 14% off the price by doing £36.99 × 0.86 = **£31.81**.
3 marks available — 1 mark for the correct method for the final answer. (You'll only get 1 mark if you give £5.18 as your answer.)

5 (a) For every 1 kg of cement, you need 3 kg of sand. So with 3½ kg of cement, you need 3 × 3½ kg = **10½ kg** of sand.
2 marks available — 1 for the right method, and 1 for the right answer.

(b) Add the ratios together and you get 1 + 3 + 2 = 6. So for every 6 kg of concrete you make, 3 kg will be sand. If you make 20 kg of concrete, you will need to multiply 3 kg of sand by 20 ÷ 6 = 3⅓; you need 3⅓ × 3 = **10 kg** of sand.
2 marks available — 1 for the method, 1 for the answer.
If RATIOS are doing your head in, get yourself some practice before the exam...

6 (a)(i) Use you calculator: 1 ÷ 16 = **0.0625**.
(ii) Multiply your answer to (a) by 100: 0.0625 × 100 = **6.25%**
1 mark available for each right answer.

(b) Either work out 6.25% of £369 (= £369 × 0.0625 = £23.06) and subtract this from £369 to give £345.94. Or reduce the price by 6.25% in one go by doing £369 × 0.9375 = **£345.94**. (Use 0.9375 because 1.0000 − 0.0625 = 0.9375).
3 marks available — 2 for the right method, and 1 for the right answer.

7 (a)

Length (*l* metres)	Tally	Frequency
0 ≤ *l* < 10		5
10 ≤ *l* < 20	||||| |||	8
20 ≤ *l* < 30	||||	4
30 ≤ *l* < 40	||||	4
40 ≤ *l* < 50			1

3 marks available — 1 mark available for each column with at least 4 correct entries.

(b) The modal class interval is the interval **0 ≤ *l* < 10**.
1 mark for choosing the correct interval.
FREQUENCY TABLES and STATISTICS — not supposed to be fun.

8 3² = 2 × 3 = 3 (too small) and 4² − 2 × 4 = 8 (too big.
So Try 3.5: 3.5² − 2 × 3.5 = 5.25 — too big.
Try 3.1: 3.1² − 2 × 3.1 = 3.41 — too small.
Try 3.2: 3.2² − 2 × 3.2 = 3.84 — too big. So solution is between 3.1 and 3.2.
Try 3.15: 3.15² − 2 × 3.15 = 3.6225 — too small, so answer is closer to 3.2. So the solution to the equation to 1 d.p. is *x* = **3.2**.
4 marks available — 3 marks for the method, and 1 for the answer.
TRIAL AND IMPROVEMENT — come on, it's a doddle if you bother to learn it.

9 There are 90 results altogether, so each result will take up 360° ÷ 90 = 4°.
3 marks available altogether — 1 mark for finding out that each result takes up 4°, and 2 marks for drawing at least 3 of the sectors *accurately*.

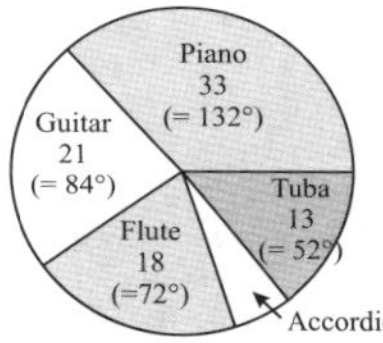

[pie chart: Piano 33 (=132°), Guitar 21 (=84°), Flute 18 (=72°), Tuba 13 (=52°), Accordion 5 (=20°)]

(b) Each person will take up 360° ÷ 180 = 2°. So 128° means 64 people. So **64 people** said they owned a dog.
2 marks available — 1 mark for saying that each person takes up 2°, 1 mark for the right answer.
Get your head round PIE CHARTS or you're throwing marks down the drain...

10 (a) Area of a trapezium = average of parallel sides × distance between them Area of *ADEB* = ((11.2 + 2.8) ÷ 2) × 12.0 = **84 cm²**
2 marks available — 1 for method and 1 for the answer.

(b) Since *DE* is ¼ of *AB*, *CD* must be ¼ of *CA*. So *DA* = 3 × *CD* = 12, and therefore *CD* = 12 ÷ 3 = **4 cm**.
3 marks available — 2 for the method and 1 for the answer.

11 (a)(i) Since the shape is a regular pentagon, the angle *AOB* must be 360° ÷ 5 = **72°**.
(ii) The angles *OAB* and *OBA* are the same. Since there are 180° in a triangle, these must equal (180° − 72°) ÷ 2 = 108° ÷ 2 = 54°. And so the angle *ABC* is 2 × 54° = **108°**
2 marks available for each part — 1 for the method and 1 for the answer.

(b) The angle S is 360° − (3 × 108°) = 360° − 324° = **36°**.
2 marks available — 1 for the method and 1 for the answer.
You need to learn all this stuff about REGULAR POLYGONS and ANGLES — there's no excuse for losing marks here.

12 (a) *x* + *x* + *x* + *x* + *x* = **5*x***. One mark for the correct answer.

(b) 2*y* + 5*y* − 4*y* + 6*y* − *y* = **8*y***.

13 (a) (*x* − 7)(*x* + 2) = *x*² − **5*x* − 14**. One mark for the correct answer.

(b) 2*x*² + 6*xy* = **2*x*(*x* + 3*y*)**.
2 marks available — 1 for each correct factor.
Got a bad feeling about this? Get that ALGEBRA learnt.

14 The area of one of the triangles is ½ × base × height = ½ × 4 × 8 = 16 cm².
So the area of the two triangles together is 2 × 16 = 32 cm².
The area of the circle = π × r² = π × 5² = π × 25 = 3.142 × 35 = 78.55 cm².
So the shaded area must be 78.55 − 32 = 46.55 = **47 cm²**, to the nearest cm².
6 marks available — 1 mark for the method of working out the area of a triangle, and 1 for getting the area of the triangles correct. Then 2 marks for the method of working out the area of a circle, and 1 mark for getting the area of the circle correct. And finally 1 mark for getting the final answer correct. (They'll let you get away with 46.55 cm² or 46.6 cm².)
That's 6 whole marks — all on AREAS.

15 (a)(i) The modal class is the one with the highest frequency; this is **20 ≤ s < 30**. One mark available.

(ii) [frequency polygon graph]

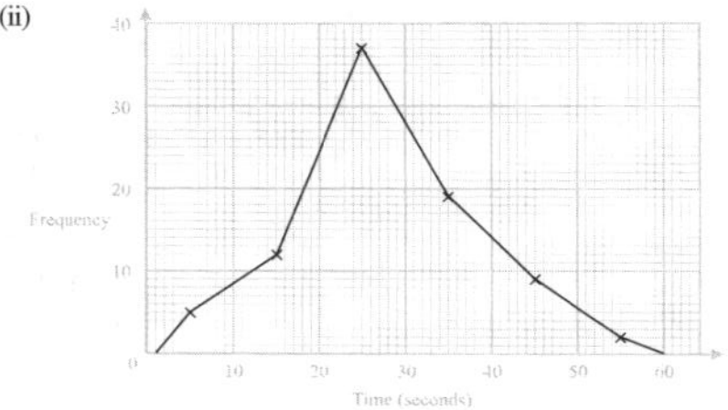

(b) To find an estimate of the mean, multiply the mid-class values by their frequencies, add up all these numbers and divide by the total number of people (=84).

Time (s seconds)	0 ≤ s < 10	10 ≤ s < 20	20 ≤ s < 30	30 ≤ s < 40	40 ≤ s < 50	50 ≤ s < 60	Totals
Mid-class value	5	15	25	35	45	55	
Number of people (frequency)	5	12	37	19	9	2	84
Mid-class value × frequency	25	180	925	665	405	110	2310

So an estimate of the mean is 2310 ÷ 84 = **28 seconds** (approx).
4 marks available — 1 for using the mid-class values, 1 for multiplying the mid-class values by the frequencies and finding the total of all these, 1 for dividing this total by the sum of the frequencies, and 1 for the right answer.
Urghh — STATISTICS.

© 2001 CGP

16(a) 1 kg = 2.2 pounds, so 1 pound = (1 ÷ 2.2) kg = 0.455 kg. And this means $\frac{1}{10}$ pound = 0.455 kg ÷ 10 = 0.0445 kg = **4.45 × 10⁻² kg**.
3 marks available — 1 for using the right method, 1 for getting the answer correct and 1 for writing it properly in standard form.

(b) 60% full = 2 tonnes. This means 1% full = 2 tonnes ÷ 60 = 0.03333 tonnes. So 100% full = 100 × 0.03333 = 3.333 tonnes = 3333 kg. This is equal to 3333 × 2.2 = 7332.6 pounds = **7330 pounds** (to 3 sig. figs.).
3 marks available — 1 for getting the right capacity, 1 for converting this correctly to pounds, and 1 for a correct final answer.
If it all went pear-shaped, get those CONVERSION FACTORS sorted out.

17(a) Triangles that have two equal sides are called *isosceles triangles*.
One mark available.

(b) If two sides are equal, then two angles are also equal, and so angle ABC is the same as angle ACB, i.e. both these angles equal x. And since the angles in a triangle add up to 180°, you know that 40 + 2x = 180. Solve this to find that **x = 70°**.
2 marks available — 1 for the correct method and 1 for the correct answer.
It's all about those ANGLE RULES.

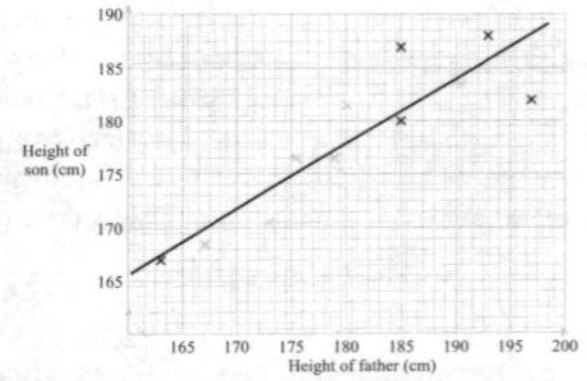

18(a) [graph]

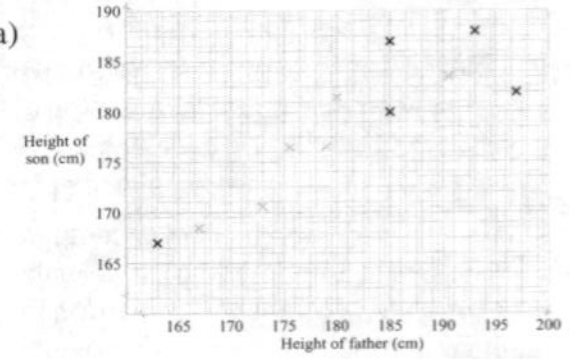

(b) 2 marks available — 1 mark for at least two points plotted correctly, and 2 marks for at least 4 points plotted correctly.

As the height of the father increases, the height of the corresponding son also increases. (In other words, *"Taller fathers generally have taller sons."*) — one mark available.

(c) 2 marks available for a straight line passing reasonably near all the points. Lose one mark for a line that doesn't fit so well.

(d) [graph] Approximately **175 cm**.

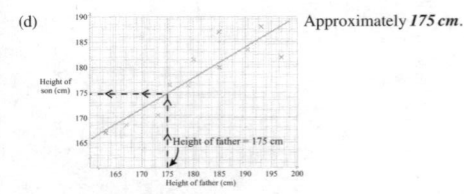

(e) [graph] Approximately **190 cm**.

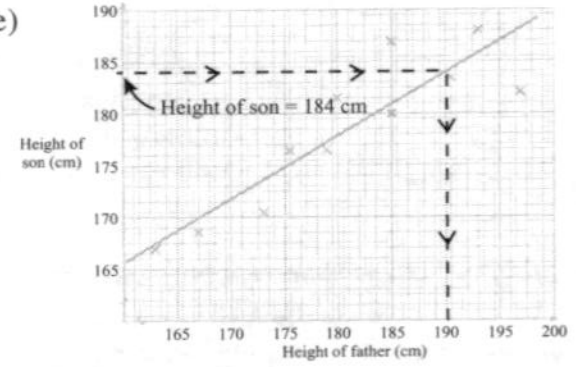

1 mark available for part (d), and 1 for part (e). Answers can be slightly different from these ones, since your line of best fit may be slightly different.
Bit of a tough one. If you got any bits wrong, go back to GRAPHS AND CHARTS.

19 (a)(i) The perimeter is the lengths of all the sides added together. This is P = (5x + 7) + (5x + 7) + 3x + 3x = **16x + 14**.
(ii) And the area is A = 3x(5x + 7) = 15x² + 21x. (You can give your answer for the area in either of these two forms.)
3 marks available — 1 each for using the correct formulas for the perimeter and area, and 1 for at least one final answer correct.

(b) Put the value P = 78 in your expression for the perimeter and you get 78 = 16x + 14. You can then rearrange this to get 16x = 64, or x = 4. Now put this value of x into the formula for the area to get A = 3 × 4 × (5 × 4 + 7) = 12 × 27 = **324 m²**.
3 marks available — 1 for using the expression for P to find x, 1 for substituting this value into the expression for A, and 1 for the final answer.
PERIMETERS AND AREAS and ALGEBRA — that's all there is to it.

20 (a)(i) The next number is (40 × 3) + 1 = **121**. One mark available.
(ii) The next term in the sequence after x is **3x + 1**.
2 marks available — 1 mark for getting the '3x part' correct, and 1 mark for getting the '+ 1' part correct.
(iii) The difference between the first two terms is 3; the difference between the next two terms is 9; the difference between the next two terms is 27 — so the difference between terms is multiplied by 3 each time. The difference between the next two terms is 81.
2 marks available for a rule that works. Get 1 mark for an incorrect rule containing at least one correct statement or idea.

(b) If you add 1 to the first 5 terms of the sequence, you get 1, 4, 9, 16, and 25 — these are the squares of 1, 2, 3, 4 and 5. So an expression for the nth term of the sequence is **n² – 1**.
2 marks available for an expression that works. Get 1 mark for an incorrect expression that contains at least one correct statement or idea.
Yeah, I agree — NUMBER PATTERNS can make your head swim.

Paper 1B

1. [pattern image]

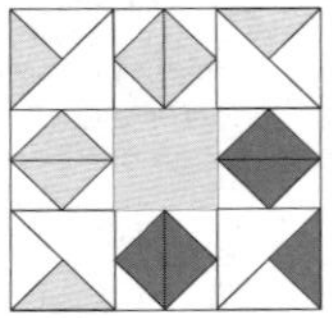

3 marks available — 1 for each of the 3 squares shaded correctly.
Can't remember how to do it? Learn your TRANSFORMATIONS.

2 (a) **6x + 5y**.
2 marks available — 1 for the '6x' bit, and 1 for the '5y' bit.
(b)(i) 3(2x − 5) = 9 means that 6x − 15 = 9. Therefore 6x = 24, and so **x = 4**.
3 marks available for the right answer — if your answer is wrong, get 1 mark for each of the underlined equations you've written down.
(ii) 9x − 15 = 4x, therefore 5x − 15 = 0, or 5x = 15. And so **x = 3**.
2 marks available for a correct answer. If your answer is wrong, get 1 mark for writing either of the underlined equations.
You won't stand a chance if you venture into that exam without your trusty REARRANGING FORMULAS skills. So tell me — do you feel lucky?

3 (a) £1 = 14 kroner, so £284 = 284 × 14 = **3976 kroner**.
2 marks available 1 for multiplying 284 by 14, and 1 mark for getting the correct answer.
(b) The shoes cost 378 kroner, so divide 378 by 14 to get the price in £. This is 378 ÷ 14 = **£27**.
2 marks for getting the right answer.
Otherwise, 1 for dividing 378 by 14.
CONVERSION FACTORS — a pain in the roubles, but they come up all the time.

4. $x = \frac{y^2 - 4}{3}$, which means that $3x = y^2 - 4$, so $y^2 = 3x + 4$, and therefore $y = \sqrt{3x + 4}$.
3 marks available — 1 for each underlined equation.

5 (a)(i) **3x + y = 65** and **x + 2y = 70**.
2 marks available — 1 for each correct equation.
(ii) Multiply the second equation by 3 to get 3x + 6y = 210. Then subtract the first equation from this new one to find 5y = 145, and so **y = 29p**.
(You could also solve this by finding x first, by multiplying the first equation from (i) by 2 (to get 6x + 2y = 130), and then subtracting the second equation to find 5x = 60, and so **x = 12**. Then substitute this value for x back into one of the equations to find y.)
3 marks available for a correct answer. If your answer is wrong, get 1 mark for each underlined equation, up to a maximum of 2.

(b)(i) If the multipack will last 8 weeks if they get through 5 packets per week, then there must be 40 packets altogether. So if they get through 8 packets per week, the multipack will last 40 ÷ 8 = **5 weeks**.
1 mark available for a correct answer.
(ii) There are 40 packets of bubble gum in the multipack. So if they get through p packets per week, the multipack will last n weeks, where n = 40 ÷ p. (Or np = 40, or **p = 40 ÷ n**.)
3 marks available for any of the underlined answers (or something equivalent, e.g. n = 40/p etc.). If your answer is wrong, get 1 mark for saying that there must be 40 packets in the multipack, and 1 for a FORMULA in which n gets smaller as p gets bigger (e.g. n = 20 ÷ p etc.).
SIMULTANEOUS EQUATIONS — it's tricky stuff, this.

6 (a) [graph]
2 marks available — 1 mark for at least 3 points plotted correctly and 2 marks for at least 6 points plotted correctly.

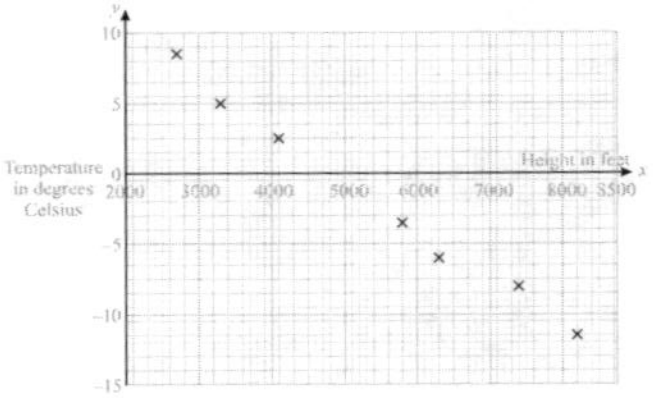

(b) As the height increases, the temperature decreases. (In other words, there is a **negative correlation** between the height and the temperature.)
One mark for expressing this idea.

(c) [graph]
One mark for a line that fits reasonably well.

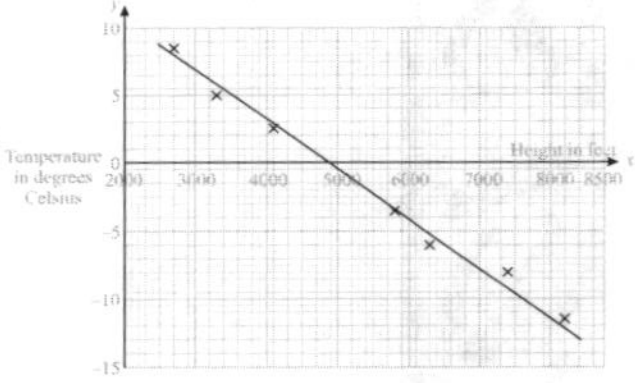

(d) *Approximately −7°C*. One mark available. (Your answer may be slightly different if you have a slightly different line of best fit.)
Oh joy of joys. STATISTICS.

7 (a) The next term is (3 × 53) + 2 = 159 + 2 = **161**.
The term after that is (3 × 161) + 2 = 483 + 2 = **485**.
One mark for each time the rule is applied correctly to work out a term. (Note you can still get 1 mark if you get the first term wrong, but then multiply that by 3 and add 2 correctly.)

(b)(i) The next term is (3 × 0) + 2 = 0 + 2 = **2**.
The term after that is (3 × 2) + 2 = 6 + 2 = **8**.
One mark for each time the rule is applied correctly. (See the note in part (a) if you got the answers wrong.)
(ii) The next term is (3 × −7) + 2 = −21 + 2 = **−19**.
The term after that is (3 × −19) + 2 = −57 + 2 = **−55**.
One mark for each time the rule is applied correctly. (See the note in part (a) if you got the answers wrong.)
Patterns in numbers? You could look in NUMBER PATTERNS...

8. Multiply the second equation by 2 to get 6x − 4y = 14. Then subtract this from the first equation in the question to find that 3x = 6, or **x = 2**. Now put this value of x back into one of the equations (for example 3x − 2y = 7) and you find that (3 × 2) − 2y = 7, i.e. 6 − 2y = 7, in other words 2y = −1. So just solve this to get **y = −0.5**.
(Or you could multiply the second equation by 3 to get 9x − 6y = 21, and then subtract this from the first equation in the question to find 2y = −1, and so y = −0.5. Then substitute this into one of the equations (for example 3x − y = 7) to find 3x + 1 = 7, i.e. 3x = 6, or simply x = 2.)
4 marks available — 2 for a correct value of x, and 2 for a correct value of y. If you got both answers wrong, get 1 mark for each of the underlined equations, up to a maximum of 3.
Suspicious? Call the Police.

© 2001 CGP

9 (a) There are 360° in a circle, so the angle for 'much happier' is
$\frac{3}{8} \times 360° = 135°$.
The angle for 'slightly happier' is $\frac{1}{3} \times 360° = 120°$.
The angle for 'slightly less happy' is $\frac{1}{4} \times 360° = 90°$.
As a check, you should work out the angle for 'much less happy' and see that you've got that angle left over at the end once you've drawn the first three 'slices of pie'. The fraction of people who were much less happy is $1 - \frac{3}{8} - \frac{1}{3} - \frac{1}{4} = \frac{24-9-8-6}{24} = \frac{1}{24}$, and so the angle for 'much less happy' is $\frac{1}{24} \times 360° = 15°$.
4 marks available — 1 for each sector with the correct angle.

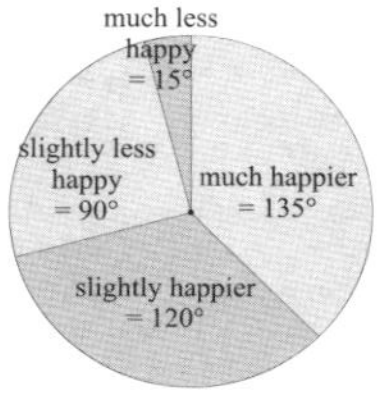

much happier = 135°
slightly happier = 120°
slightly less happy = 90°
much less happy = 15°

(b) If 48 people took part in the survey, then $\frac{3}{8} \times 48 = 18$ people were much happier.
2 marks available — 1 mark for the method and 1 for a correct final answer.
Forget the "360° around a point" rule and you're in big trouble.

10 Draw at least 6 extra shapes.

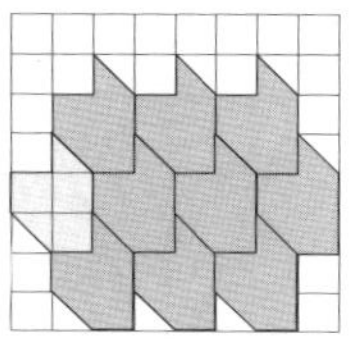

3 marks available — 1 for drawing the same shape as marked in the diagram at least once somewhere, 1 for drawing at least 3 shapes in correct positions, and 1 for at least 6 shapes correct.

11 (a) $\frac{5}{6} - \frac{3}{5} = \frac{(5 \times 5) - (3 \times 6)}{30} = \frac{25-18}{30} = \frac{7}{30}$.
2 marks available for a correct answer. If your answer is wrong, get one mark for using a common denominator of 30.

(b) $\frac{2}{7} \times \frac{3}{8} = \frac{6}{56} = \frac{3}{28}$.
2 marks available for a correct answer. If your answer is wrong, get one mark for the underlined fraction.
If you're a bit rusty, practise your FRACTIONS. You know it makes sense.

12(a)(i) $x^5 \times x^7 = x^{12}$. (Add the indices if the numbers are multiplied.)
1 mark for a correct answer.

(ii) $\frac{6y^7}{2y^2} = 3y^5$. (Subtract the indices (of y) if the numbers are divided.)
1 mark for a correct answer.

(b) $4t + 12 < 4$ means that $4t < -8$, and so $t < -2$.
2 marks available for a correct answer. If your answer is wrong, get 1 mark for the underlined equation.

(c) $d = \frac{u+v}{7}$, and so $7d = u+v$, which means $u = 7d - v$.
2 marks available for a correct answer. If your answer is wrong, get 1 mark for the underlined equation.
If you didn't get 6 marks, it's more ALGEBRA revision for you.

13(a)(i)

x	0	1.5	3
	1	3	6

One mark for getting both entries in the table correct.
(ii) See graph below. One mark for the correct straight line.

(b)(i)

x	0	0.5	1	1.5	2	2.5	3
	0	0.25	1	2.25	4	6.25	9

2 marks available — 1 for at least 2 correct entries in the table, and 2 marks for all 4 correct.
(ii) See graph below.
2 marks available — 1 mark for at least 3 points plotted correctly, and 2 marks for 5 points plotted correctly.

(a & b)(ii)
$A = x^2$
$A = 2x$

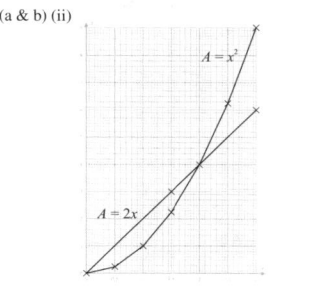

(c) $x = 2$. One mark available.
PLOTTING GRAPHS — take your time and do it neatly.

14 (a) The line in bold is the locus of all points equidistant from A and D.
2 marks available — 1 for a straight line, 1 if it's the correct line.

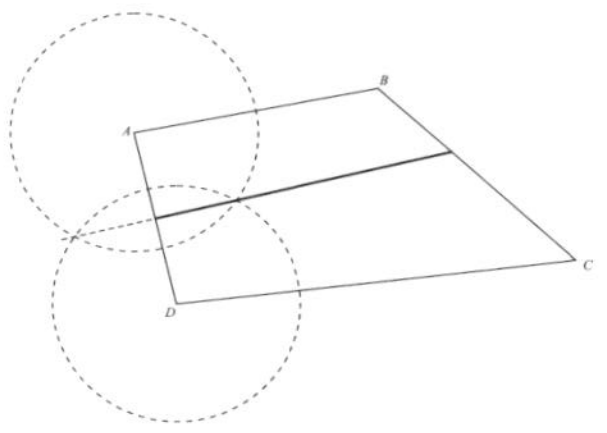

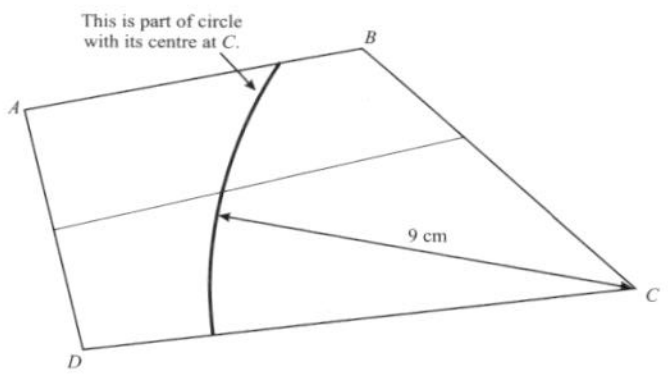

This is part of circle with its centre at C.

(b) The arc in bold is the locus of all points exactly 18 m from C.
2 marks available — 1 mark for drawing part of a circle with its centre at C, and 1 mark for a diameter of 9 cm.

(c) The line in bold is the required line.
One mark available.

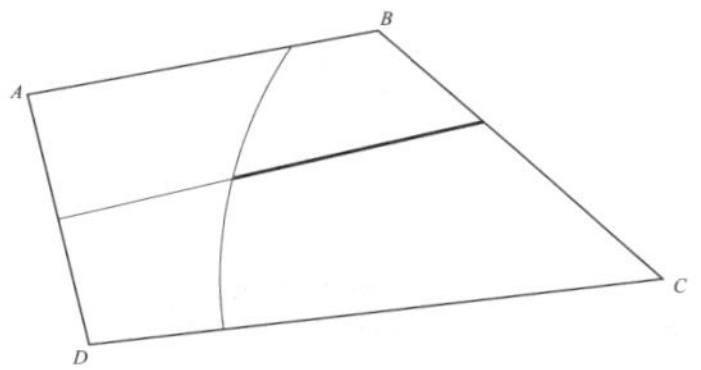

15(a)(i) The angle marked x is $180° - 38° = 142°$.
(ii) There are 180° on a straight line, so the angles DCE and BCD must add up to 180°.
1 mark for part (i), and 1 for part (ii).

(b)(i) $y = 38°$.
(ii) *The angles ABC and BCD are alternate angles, and so must be equal.*
1 mark for part (i), and 1 for part (ii).
If you just don't get it, you need to revise GEOMETRY.

16(a) The triangles are similar, so XYZ is an enlargement of ABC, and all the sides are multiplied by the same scale factor. To work out the scale factor, divide the length YZ by length BC, i.e. $12.8 \text{ cm} \div 3.2 \text{ cm} = 4$. So the scale factor is 4. Therefore $p = 4 \times 4.1 \text{ cm} = 16.4 \text{ cm}$.
3 marks available — 1 for finding the correct scale factor, 1 for multiplying 4.1 cm by 4, and 1 for a correct final answer.

(b) q is given by $22.4 \text{ cm} \div 4 = 5.6 \text{ cm}$.
2 marks available — 1 for dividing 22.4 cm by 4, and 1 for a correct final answer.
There's a heap of stuff on this in TRANSFORMATIONS.

17(a)(i)

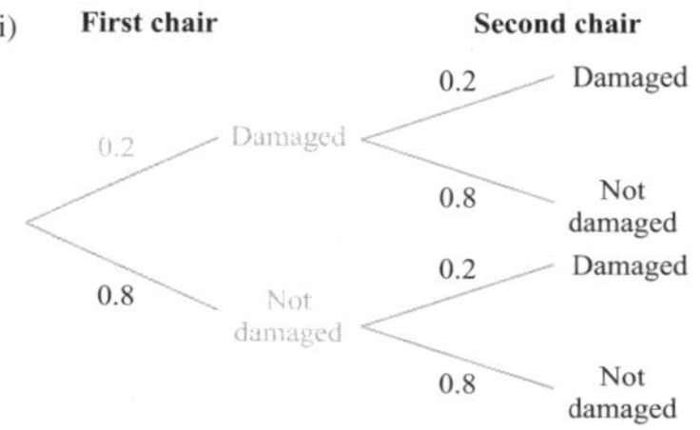

First chair	Second chair
0.2 Damaged	0.2 Damaged
	0.8 Not damaged
0.8 Not damaged	0.2 Damaged
	0.8 Not damaged

2 marks available — 1 for at least 2 of the probabilities entered correctly, 2 for all 5 correct.

(ii) The probability that at least 1 of the 2 chairs is not damaged is $(0.8 \times 0.8) + (0.8 \times 0.2) + (0.2 \times 0.8) = 0.64 + 0.16 + 0.16 = 0.96$.
3 marks available — 1 mark for including the (0.8×0.8) term, 1 for including either the (0.8×0.2) term or the (0.2×0.8) term, and 1 for a correct answer.
(Or you could work this out as $1 - $ (probability that both are damaged). this equals $1 - (0.2 \times 0.2) = 1 - 0.04 = 0.96$.
If you do it this way, get 1 mark for the method and 1 for the answer expressed.)

(b)(i) They can expect $(0.2 \times 50) = 10$ chairs to be damaged.
2 marks available — 1 mark for the method and 1 for the answer.
(ii) *This answer is only approximate because expected values are only a guess of what might happen in the future, and the actual figure could be slightly higher or lower than the expected value.*
See PROBABILITY if this makes no sense at all.

18(a)(i) The median length is the one in the middle. There are 24 worms, so if you lined all the lengths up in order, the middle ones would be the 12th and 13th worms which are both 7 cm. So the median length is *7 cm*.
(ii) The range of the lengths is the longest minus the shortest.
This is $9 \text{ cm} - 5 \text{ cm} = 4 \text{ cm}$.
One mark available for each part correct.
(iii) There are seven worms and the median is 8 cm, so you need 3 worms longer than 8 cm and 3 shorter. And since the range is 10 cm, the difference between the longest and the shortest must be 10 cm. *One possible list of values would be: 5, 6, 7, 8, 9, 10, 15*. (There are 3 numbers bigger than 8, and 3 numbers smaller. And the difference between the biggest and the smallest is 10. (All measurements are in cm.))
2 marks available — 1 mark if the median of your list is 8 cm, and 1 if the range of your list is 10 cm.

(b)(i) Just plot the points from the table on the graph and then draw a curve of best fit through them. (The trick is to realise that 4 squares are 0.1 g on the horizontal axis).

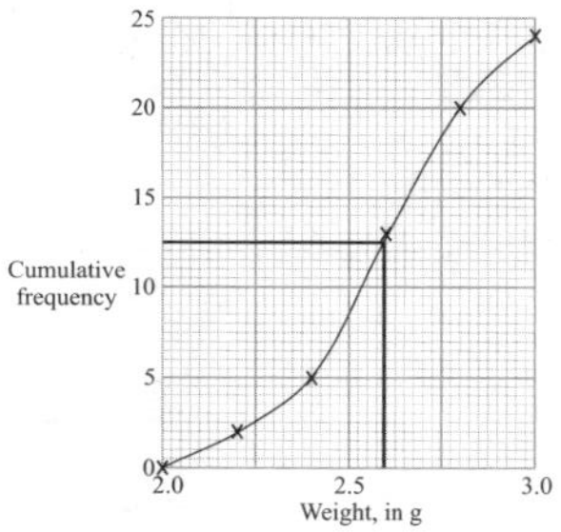

3 marks for correctly plotting the points and drawing a line through the points.
Lose a mark if line has not been drawn through the points. Lose marks for inaccuracy.
(ii) Median is *2.6*.
There are 24 worms. The median is halfway between the 12th and 13th worm. The middle is halfway between the 12th and 13th worm, i.e. 12.5 (Add 1 to the number of worms and divide by 2). So draw a horizontal line from 12.5 on the vertical axis and find what reading this gives for the weight.
Award 2 marks for correct method and answer.
Lose a mark if answer does not round to 2.6.
If this stuff's making you sweat, there's only one thing to do — more STATS.

© 2001 CGP

Paper 2A

1 (a) $9 \times 9 = 81$ (b) $7 \times 7 \times 7 = 343$ (c) $3 \times 3 \times 3 \times 3 = 81$
  (d) $4 \times 10 \times 10 = 4 \times 1000 = 4000$
  (e) $2.6 \times 10 \times 10 = 2.6 \times 100 = 260$
  1 mark for each correct answer.
  5 marks up for grabs — get those POWER RULES learned.

2 (a) Modal reason is *"The roads were flooded"* — the section extending through the largest angle, or the reason with the highest frequency.
  1 mark for correct answer — know your averages!
  (b) Angle swept through by 'Tank' excuse is $48°$. Total angle = $360°$.
  Fraction of employees held up by tank = $\frac{48}{360} \Rightarrow \frac{48}{360} \times \frac{30}{30} = \frac{2}{15} \times \frac{30}{30} = \frac{4}{15}$
  3 marks available — 1 for correct measurement of angle, 1 for correct fraction ($\frac{2}{15}$), 1 for correct answer.
  Don't think of ricking these excuses to get out of your exam — it won't work.

3 (a) Area of rectangle = 2× area of triangle.
  Area of triangle = ½ × base × perpendicular height
  = ½ × 5 × 2 = 5.
  ∴ Area of rectangle = 2×5 = **10 cm²**
  2 marks available — 1 for a valid method, 1 for right answer.
  (b) An isosceles triangle is symmetrical about 1 or more axes:

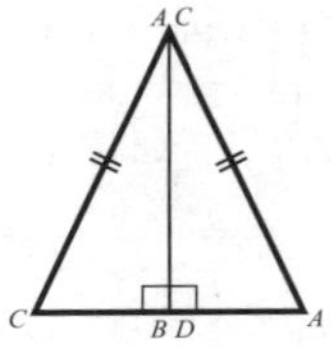

  (So it has at least two sides the same length.)
  2 marks available — 1 for correct assembly, 1 for correct labelling.

4 Work this out on your calculator:
  $19.8 \times 48.3 \div (23.46 - 5.17) = $ **52.3**
  Or, if you don't have a 'brackets' button: $23.46 - 5.17 = 18.29$
  $\Rightarrow 19.8 \times 48.3 = 956.34 \Rightarrow 956.34 \div 18.29 = 52.3$
  (3 significant figures means you round your answer to leave just 3 digits. For larger numbers, you may have to stick some noughts in to make it the right size.)
  3 marks available — 1 for the right method, 1 for the right answer, 1 for the correct degree of accuracy. (If you scribble some of your working down, you could still get the method marks even if your answer's wrong.)
  You'll lose marks here if you get the wrong number of SIGNIFICANT FIGURES.

5 (a) Draw a line up from £4.75, then across from where it meets the conversion line. Read off the value of drachmas where your line falls. £4.75 = **2850D**
  2 marks available — 1 for the right method, and 1 for the answer.

a)

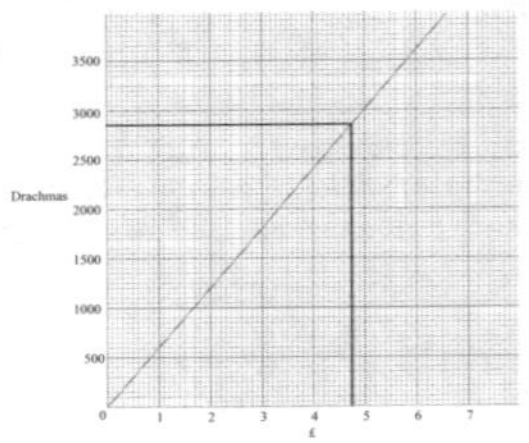

b)

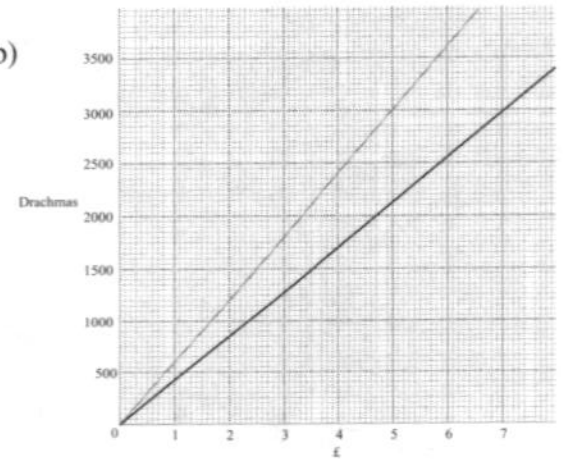

(b) Your line should pass through (£0, 0D), (£1, 420D), (£5, 2100D).
3 marks are available — 1 for the graph passing through each of these points (proving you've worked out more than one exact point on the line).
If you didn't get it quite right, do a few more PLOTTING GRAPHS questions.

6 (a)

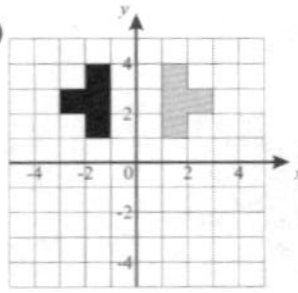

(b)

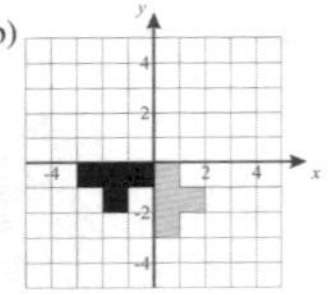

2 marks available for each part — 1 for each correct type of translation, 1 for each correct translation.

(c)

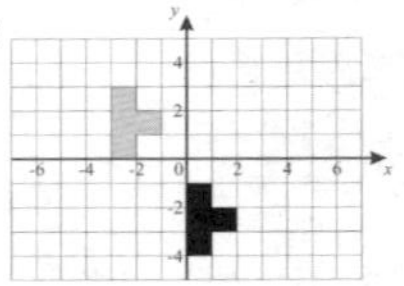

1 mark for correct answer.
Aaah — THE FOUR TRANSFORMATIONS. Bless their cotton socks.

7 (a) **6n**
  1 mark for correct answer — a multiple of the cost denoted by n.
  (b) $6 \times 9(n+2) = 54(n+2)$ or $54n + 108$
  1 mark for multiplying the formula by the correct number.

(c) (i) 6 pairs socks + 6 pairs shoes = $6n + 54n + 108 = 228$
    $60n + 108 = 228$
    so a pair of socks costs **£2 per pair**.
(ii) $60n + 108 = 228$
    $60n = 228 - 108 = 120$
    $n = \frac{120}{60} = 2$
There are 2 marks for forming the equation — one for getting the right bits together, and another for simplifying it.
There are 2 more easy marks for going one step further and solving it — 1 for your working and 1 for the right answer.
More ALGEBRA.

8 (a) $x^2(7x^2 - 2x + 3)$ b) $(6x+3)(2x-4)$
  $\Rightarrow 7x^2(x^2) - 2x(x^2) + 3(x^2)$ $\Rightarrow (6x \times 2x) - (6x \times 4) + (3 \times 2x) - (3 \times 4)$
  $\Rightarrow 7x^4 - 2x^3 + 3x^2$ $\Rightarrow 12x^2 - 24x + 6x - 12$
  $\Rightarrow 12x^2 - 18x - 12$
There are 2 marks available for part (a) — 1 for correct expansion, and 1 for simplification (grouping the similar terms).
There are 3 marks for part (b) — 1 for the method of multiplying out, 1 for the method of simplification, and 1 for the correct answer.
Yet more ALGEBRA.

9 (a) Volume = length × width × height = $24 \times 16 \times 3.5 = $ **1344 m³**
2 marks available — 1 for correct method, 1 for correct answer.
(b) New volume = $24 \times 16 \times 5.4 = 2073.6$ m³
Increase in volume = $2073.6 - 1344 = 729.6$ m³
Percentage increase in volume = $\frac{729.6}{1344} \times 100 = $ **54.3%**
3 marks available — 1 mark for calculating increase in volume, 1 for correct method to find % increase, 1 mark for correct answer (must be to 3 sig. figs.).

10 (a) Appropriate degree of accuracy is the same as the values you've been given to work with — i.e. 2 d.p., or 3 s.f.
New P.B. is found by: $3.80 \times 1.06 = 4.028$
= **4.03 m**
3 marks available here — 1 for method, 1 for correct answer, and 1 for appropriate degree of accuracy.
(b) Measured increase = $4.81 - 4.24 = 0.57$ m
Percentage increase = $\frac{0.57}{4.24} \times 100 = $ **13.44%** $\left(=13\frac{47}{106}\right)$
3 marks available — 1 for the increase, 1 for the method and 1 for the answer.
PERCENTAGES again — no rest for the wicked.

11 (a) SOHCAHTOA $\sin A = \frac{Opposite}{Hypotenuse} = \frac{8}{14}$
    $\Rightarrow A = \sin^{-1}\left(\frac{8}{14}\right) = $ **34.85°**
3 marks available — 1 for using trig, 1 for right method, 1 for right answer.

(b) $\cos 46° = \frac{Adjacent}{Hypotenuse} = \frac{AD}{14}$
    $\Rightarrow AD = 14\cos 46° = 14 \times 0.695 = $ **9.73 cm**
3 marks available — 1 for using trig, 1 for method, 1 for answer.
TRIGONOMETRY — SIN, COS, TAN.

12 (a)

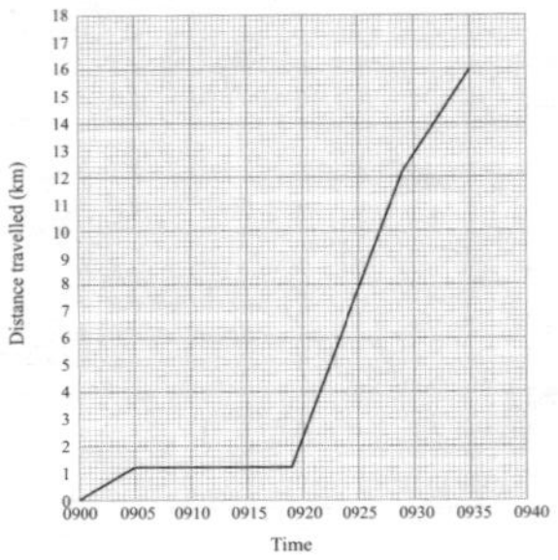

$Speed = \frac{Distance}{Time}$

$\Rightarrow d = st$ 5 mins $\Rightarrow d = st$ 14 mins
$\Rightarrow d = \frac{14.4}{60} \times 5 = 1.2$ km $\Rightarrow d = 0 \times 14 = 0$ km

11 km   6 mins
$\Rightarrow t = \frac{d}{s}$ $\Rightarrow d = st$
$\Rightarrow t = \frac{11}{14.4} = \frac{11}{14.4} \times 1 \text{ hr} = 10$ mins $\Rightarrow d = 6 \times \frac{38}{60} = 3.8$ km

4 marks available — 2 for working — 1 for at least 2 correct calculations, 2nd for all correct. 2 for graph — 1 for at least 2 points plotted correctly, 2nd for complete consistency with earlier calculations.
TRAVEL GRAPHS aren't that nasty really. They're just misunderstood.

(b) At 0925, Minjita is **7.8 km** from home. (Read it from the graph.)
1 mark available for an answer between 7.7 and 7.9 km.

13 (i) **0.7**. P(all events) – P(slug) – P(beetle) = $1 - 0.2 - 0.1 = 0.7$.
2 marks for the correct answer, otherwise 1 mark for the right method.
(ii) **2 beetles**. $20 \times $ P(beetle) = $20 \times 0.1 = 2$.
2 marks for the right answer, otherwise 1 mark for the correct method.
Altogether now: "I love PROBABILITY questions..."

14 (a) If $AB = AC$, triangle is isosceles, so
$x° = \frac{1}{2} \times (180° - 50°) = \frac{1}{2} \times 130° = $ **65°**
(b) From angles on a line, $y° = 180° - x° = 180° - 65° = $ **115°**
3 marks to get here — 1 for each correct answer, and 1 for working.

15 As shapes are similar, angles remain unchanged, and so sides all change by same scale factor: $6 \div 9 = \frac{2}{3}$, so $\frac{2}{3} \times 15 = $ **10 cm**
2 marks available, one for recognising significance of similarity, 1 for answer.
Oooh — there go those TRANSFORMATIONS again...

16 (a)(i) Median is ½(n + 1)th value when arranged in size order.
½(n + 1) = 4.
4th time when arranged in chronological order is **8:31am**.
1 mark for answer.
(ii) Number of minutes late for each employee:
P = 1   R = 9   S = 3   V = 6
Mean = $(1 + 9 + 3 + 6) \div 4 = \frac{19}{4} = $ **4.75 minutes late**
4 minutes 45 seconds.
3 marks available — 1 for working out latenesses, 1 for correct method for mean, and 1 for a correct final answer.
Bonus question for 0 marks: come up with a better pun than this: "That was a MEAN question."

© 2001 CGP

(b) $4(x+8) < x-1$
$4x + 32 < x - 1$
$3x < -33$
$x < -11$
3 marks available — 2 for method, 1 for answer.

(c)(i) [graph showing two lines intersecting]

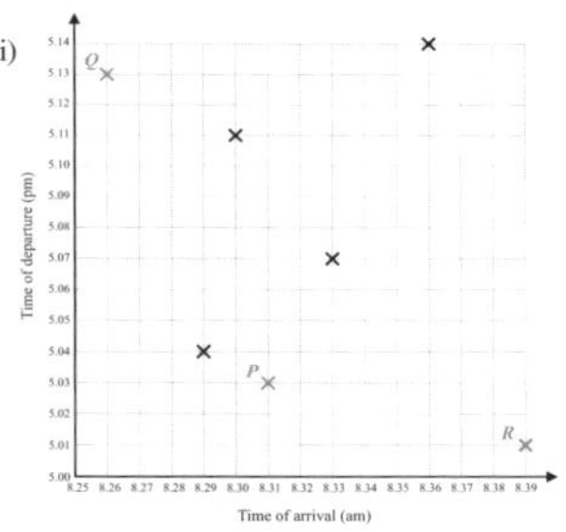

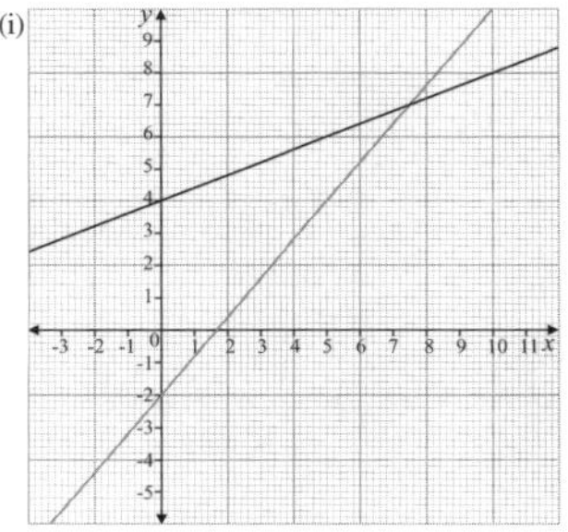

(ii) $x = 7.5, y = 7$
Read the answer straight from the graph.
(The coordinates of the point of intersection.)
Algebraic proof: $5y = 6x - 10 \Rightarrow 0 = 4x - 30 \Rightarrow 5y = 2(7.5) + 20 = 15 + 20$
$5y = 2x + 20$ $4x = 30$ $5y = 35$
$x = \frac{30}{4} = 7.5$ $y = \frac{35}{5} = 7$
2 marks available — one for each coordinate.
Blimey — what a question.

19 (a) n^{th} term given by $2n$. 1 mark for correct answer.
(b) n^{th} term given by $2 + 3(n-1)$ or $3n - 1$. 1 mark for correct answer.
(c) n^{th} term given by n^2. 1 mark for correct answer.
(d) n^{th} term given by $3n^2$. 2 marks available — 1 for recognising there are two different operations to get the next number in the sequence, 1 mark for correct answer.

20(a) Median time found by taking ½(n + 1)th value = ½(35 + 1) = 18th value.
Just draw a line from 18 on the vertical axis to the curve, then read off the corresponding time. **Median = 17 mins.** 1 mark available for correct answer.

(b) [cumulative frequency graph]

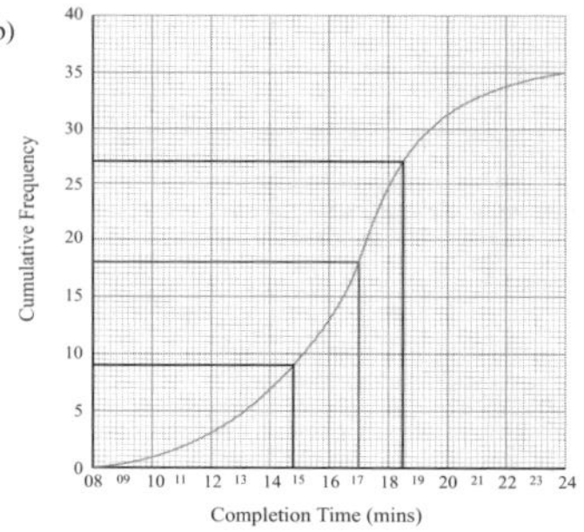

Upper quartile found from ¾(n+1)th value, lower quartile from ¼(n+1)th value. UQ = ¾(36)th = 27th value = 18.5. LQ = ¼(36)th = 9th value = 14.8. So IQR = 18.5 − 14.8 = **3.7 minutes**.
3 marks available — 1 for the lower quartile, 1 for the upper quartile and 1 for the correct final answer.
CUMULATIVE FREQUENCY CURVES.

Most employees are dedicated and make up the time by which they were late. R is the odd one out from the sample, with a deficit of 8 mins. The company is overall, making a 'profit' on time worked by their employees. There is very little correlation between the plotted points.

1 mark for a sensible conclusion incorporating 1 or more points from above.

17 (a) Number plain = ⅔ × number milk, so if plain = P and milk = M, P = 2 parts, M = 5 parts so P(P) = ²/₇. There are 329 boxes so ²/₇ × 329 = **94**.
3 marks available — 1 working out proportions correctly (2:5), 1 for getting probability fraction, and 1 for final answer.

(b) Best way to solve this is with a tree diagram, but working is the same whether it's drawn or not (and there's not really room). Here's what it would be:

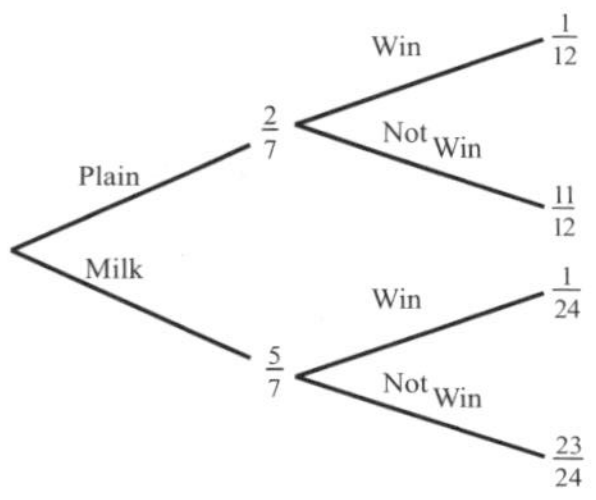

[tree diagram with Plain 2/7, Milk 5/7 branches, Win/Not Win with 1/12, 11/12, 1/24, 23/24]

So the sum of the probabilities of the winning roots is
(²/₇ × ¹/₁₂) + (⁵/₇ × ¹/₂₄) = ⁹/₁₆₈ = ³/₅₆
3 marks available — 1 for calculating each probability, and 1 for the final answer.
THE PROBABILITY of this coming up in your exam is 1.

18(a)(i) $4x = \frac{1}{8}$
$\Rightarrow x = \frac{1}{8} \times \frac{1}{4} = \frac{1}{8 \times 4} = \frac{1}{32}$
1 mark available for correct answer.

(ii) $2x^2 - 6x + 4 = 0$
$\Rightarrow 2$ ways to solve — FACTORISE, or FORMULA
$\Rightarrow$ Factorises to: $2(x-2)(x-1) = 0 \Rightarrow x = 2, 1$
$\Rightarrow$ OR $ax^2 + bx + c = 0 \Rightarrow a = 2, b = -6, c = 4$
$\Rightarrow x = \frac{-b \pm \sqrt{b^2 - 4ac}}{2a} = \frac{6 \pm \sqrt{(-6)^2 - (4 \times 2 \times 4)}}{2 \times 2} = \frac{6 \pm \sqrt{4}}{4} = 2, 1$
2 marks — one for method, 1 for answer.

Paper 2B

1 (a)(i) $24 \div 2 = 12$, $12 \div 2 = 6$
1 mark for getting both correct.
(ii) Divide the term by 2 to find the next term.
1 mark for correct answer.

(b)(i) **31**. 1 mark.
(ii) To get the nth term, add 2^{n-1} to the (n − 1)th term (in other words: double and add 1)
2 marks for correct answer. Otherwise, get 1 mark for something like "add twice the difference between the previous two terms."

(c)(i) $\frac{1}{3n-1}$
2 marks for correct answer. Otherwise, get 1 mark for getting n or $(n-1)$ somewhere.
Tricky stuff — check out NUMBER PATTERNS and FINDING THE NTH TERM.

(ii) $\frac{4-n}{5}$
2 marks for correct answer. Otherwise, get 1 mark for the right answer but not written in standard form (eg 32×10^5)

2 (a) $a \times b = 8 \times 10^2 \times 4 \times 10^3 = 32 \times 10^5 = 3.2 \times 10^6$, in standard form.
2 marks for correct answer. Otherwise, get 1 mark for the right answer but not written in standard form (eg 32×10^5)

(b) $a + b = (8 \times 10^2) + (4 \times 10^3) = 800 + 4000 = 4800$
2 marks for correct answer. Otherwise, get 1 mark for the correct answer in the standard form (4.8×10^3), or other equivalent version.
STANDARD INDEX FORM — bit fiddly, but if you can do one, you can do 'em all.

3 (a) 5
145 ÷ 34 = 4.3, and you round up to 5, because he needs to carry all of his CDs, even if it means the last box isn't full.
2 marks for correct answer. Otherwise, 1 mark for correct method.

(b) £13 × 5 = **£65**.
2 marks for correct answer. Otherwise, 1 mark if method was correct but the answer used from part a) was wrong.

(c) **9** (because 4 × 34 = 136 and 145 − 136 = 9)
2 marks for correct answer. Otherwise, 1 mark for correct method.
If you made a daft mistake, you need to try a few more of these.

4 (a) Probabilities add up to 1, so
P(not cola or strawberry) = 1 − 0.2 − 0.3 = 0.5
...and the probability of getting blackcurrant or orange is equal, so just halve what's left:
P(orange) = 0.5 / 2 = **0.25**
2 marks available for correct answer, otherwise 1 for method

(b) P(strawberry) = $\frac{\text{no. of strawberry sweets}}{\text{total no. of sweets}} = \frac{\text{no. of strawberry sweets}}{80} = 0.3$
So no. of strawberry sweets = 80 × 0.3 = **24**
2 marks available for correct answer, otherwise 1 for method.
Just a plain, boring PROBABILITY question.

5 (a) $2x - 5 = 45 \Rightarrow 2x = 50 \Rightarrow x = 25$
2 marks available for correct answer, otherwise 1 for correct method.

(b) $2x + 3 = 51 - 4x \Rightarrow 6x = 48 \Rightarrow x = 8$
2 marks: $6x = 48$ gets 1 mark; $x = 8$ gets both marks.
Even more ALGEBRA — just grit your teeth and learn it.

6 (a) 2 marks for drawing one of the planes shown below.
Lose 1 mark if the plane drawn isn't quite symmetrical.

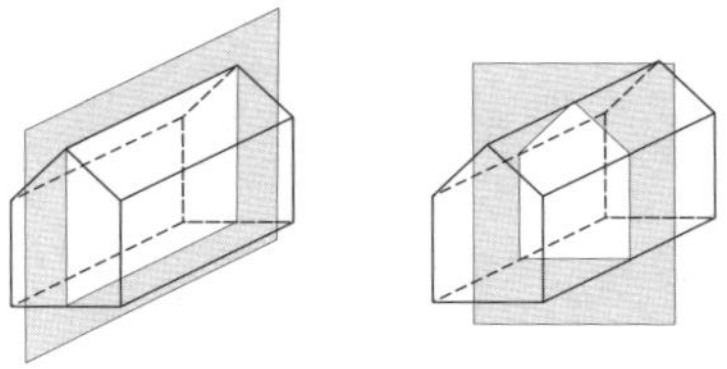

[two diagrams of 3D prism shapes with plane sections]

(b) There are 360° in a quadrilateral, so:
$x = 360 - 97 - 41 - 72 = 150°$
2 marks available for correct answer, otherwise 1 mark for method.

(c) There are 360° around a point, and it's a regular polygon, so it's just: $y = 360 \div 5 = 72°$
2 marks available for correct answer, otherwise 1 mark for method.
GEOMETRY's the bit to revise if you're struggling with this.

7 For step n, number of triangles is 4^{n-1}
2 marks available for the correct answer, otherwise 1 mark for spotting the multiple of 4 but not expressing it correctly.

8 (a) Probabilities add up to 1, so:
$1 - 0.3 - 0.1 = 0.6$ gets 1 mark

(b) P(not passing Lisa) = 1 − P(passing Lisa)
$1 - 0.3 = 0.7$
2 marks for correct answer, otherwise 1 for method.

(c) P(meeting Lisa on Tuesday and Wednesday) =
P(Lisa takes Route B) × P(Lisa takes Route C) = 0.1×0.6 = **0.06**
2 marks available for correct answer, otherwise 1 mark for correct method.
*Hacked off with PROBABILITY?
Tough toenails, you've gotta do it.*

9 (a) $x = 2, y = 3$
Second Eqn × 2 gives $14y - 4x = 34$.
Adding to Eqn 1 gives $19y = 57$,
so $y = 3$. $x = (23 - 5y)/4$, which gives $x = 2$.
4 marks for correct answer, otherwise, 3 marks are available for using the correct method throughout (e.g. marks would be given for the underlined statements above.)

(b) $z > -6$
$-6z - 5 < -2z + 19 \Rightarrow -19 - 5 < 6z - 2z \Rightarrow -24 < 4z \Rightarrow -6 < z$.
2 marks for the correct answer. Otherwise, 1 mark for correct method.
6 marks — you can't afford to throw away that many marks. Make sure you can do all this SIMULTANEOUS EQUATIONS and INEQUALITIES stuff.

10 Gradient = change in y ÷ change in x
= (60 − 0) ÷ (35 − 15) = 60 ÷ 20 = 3.
To find equation of the line, start with general equation of a line:
y = mx + c.
m = 3 (you've just worked that out), so that gives: $y = 3x + c$.
To find c, substitute in the coordinates of any point on the line, eg (15, 0). Substituting in gives: $0 = (3 \times 15) + c$, ie $c = -45$.
So the equation of the line is: $y = 3x - 45$
4 marks available for correct answer. Otherwise, 2 marks for correctly using graph to find that the gradient m = 3 and 1 mark for using the graph to find the value of c (from y = mx + c).
Phew — see FINDING THE EQUATION OF A STRAIGHT LINE.

© 2001 CGP

11 $a_1 = 4$, so $b_1 = 3 - 5a_1 = -17$. b_1 isn't less than −60, so carry on:
$a_2 = 7$, so $b_2 = 3 - 5a_2 = -32$. b_2 isn't less than −60, so carry on:
$a_3 = 10$, so $b_3 = 3 - 5a_3 = -47$. b_3 isn't less than −60, so carry on:
$a_4 = 13$, so $b_4 = 3 - 5a_4 = -62$. b_4 is now less than −60, so stop.
Award 1 mark for each correct number. If answer is correct, award 6 marks. But lose 2 marks if an extra number is given at the end (i.e. decision box is not used correctly).
Urk — a bit of everything in there. You need plenty of practice at SUBSTITUTING INTO FORMULAS and INEQUALITIES.

12 (a) **B**   (b) **A**   (c) **C**   (d) **D**
4 marks available — 1 mark for each correct answer.
Not sure what's going on? Have a butcher's at GRAPHS AND CHARTS.

13(a) $x = (180° − 44°)/2$ (since triangle BCD is isosceles)
so $x = $ **68°**
2 marks for correct answer, otherwise 1 for underlined statement.

(b) $y = 180° − (180° − x) − a$
So $y = $ **68°** $− a$
2 marks for correct answer.

(c) AD = DC means triangle is isosceles, so y = a
i.e. $a = 68° − a$
$a = $ **34°**
2 marks for correct answer, otherwise 1 for underlined statement.
It's only ANGLES — they won't bite.

14(a) Cost of 1 litre of petrol is £2 ÷ 50 = £0.04 = 4p
So cost of 20 litres of petrol is 4 × 20 = **80p**
2 marks for correct answer. Otherwise, 1 mark for method.

(b) Cost of petrol per litre is £17 ÷ 20 = £0.85 = **85p**
2 marks for correct answer. Otherwise, 1 mark for method.
This stuff's pretty easy, but don't go making silly mistakes.

15(a)(i) 1 mark for $6x + 10$ (or an equivalent expression)
(ii) 1 mark for $(4+x)(1+2x)$ (or an equivalent expression, such as $2x^2 + 9x + 4$)

(b) $(4+x)(1+2x) = 15$, multiplying out brackets gives
$4 + 9x + 2x^2 = 15$
which gives $2x^2 + 9x − 11 = 0$
3 marks for correct answer. Otherwise, 1 mark for each method stage as underlined.
BASIC ALGEBRA, REARRANGING FORMULAS and SOLVING EQUATIONS.

16(a) $b^2 − 4ac = 2^2 − (4 × 3 × −8) = 4 − −96 = $ **100**
2 marks for correct answer. Otherwise, 1 for method.

(b) $\dfrac{-b \pm \sqrt{b^2 - 4ac}}{2a} = \dfrac{-2 \pm \sqrt{100}}{2 \times 3} = \dfrac{-2 \pm 10}{6} = \dfrac{4}{6}$ and -2

3 marks available for correct answers.
Otherwise, award 2 marks for correct method.
See SUBSTITUTING INTO FORMULAS if you cockled that one up.

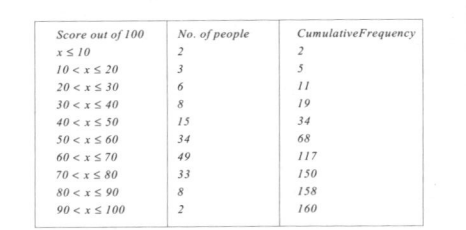

17(a)
Score out of 100	No. of people	Cumulative Frequency
$x \le 10$	2	2
$10 < x \le 20$	3	5
$20 < x \le 30$	6	11
$30 < x \le 40$	8	19
$40 < x \le 50$	15	34
$50 < x \le 60$	34	68
$60 < x \le 70$	49	117
$70 < x \le 80$	33	150
$80 < x \le 90$	8	158
$90 < x \le 100$	2	160

2 marks for getting them all right. Or 1 mark for getting at least 5 right.
If you didn't get that bit right, hang your head in shame.

(b)
Score out of 100	No. of people	Cumulative Frequency
$x \le 10$	2	2
$10 < x \le 20$	3	5
$20 < x \le 30$	6	11
$30 < x \le 40$	8	19
$40 < x \le 50$	15	34
$50 < x \le 60$	34	68
$60 < x \le 70$	49	117
$70 < x \le 80$	33	150
$80 < x \le 90$	8	158
$90 < x \le 100$	2	160

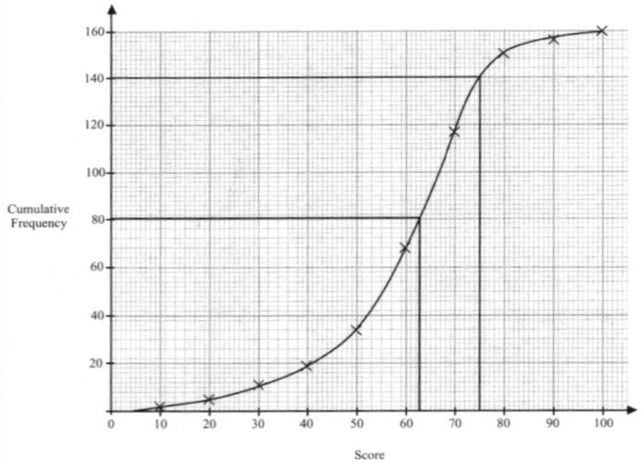

3 marks for plotting all the points right and getting a nice smooth curve. Lose 1 mark for drawing a naff curve, and lose another if you plotted more than three of the points wrong.

(c) Using the graph, median score is **63**.
Award 1 mark for answers in range 62 – 64.

(d) Using the graph, estimated number of people scoring less than 75 is **140**.
Award 1 mark for answers in range 138 – 142.
Yeah, I agree — CUMULATIVE FREQUENCY CURVES are a pain in the...

18(a) 3 marks available for correct answer **14 km**.
1 mark for correctly measuring 2.8cm (award mark for 2.7 to 2.9 cm)
1 mark for method 5 × 2.8 = 14 km. (Lose 2 marks if units are not given.)

(b) **243°** — 2 marks available for correct answer. Accept 1 degree either side. Lose 1 mark if units are not given.
BEARINGS — always measure clockwise from the north line.

19

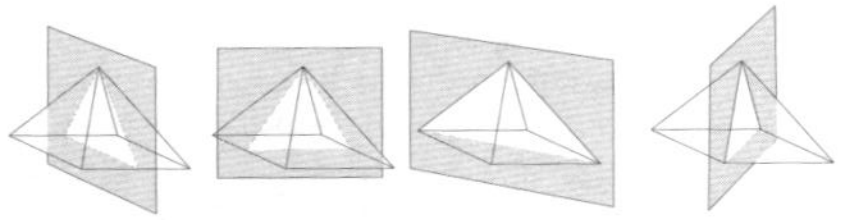

2 marks each for any two of these (total 4 marks). Lose one mark for each scrappily drawn diagram. No marks for neat drawing of a plane of symmetry in the wrong place.
SYMMETRY looks like a load of pictures, but you've still got to be able to do it.

20(a) 100 − 44 − 30 − 10 = **16%** — 1 mark for correct answer.
(b) 250 × 30/100 = **75** — 1 mark for correct answer.
(c) 16/100 × 360 = **57.6** — 2 marks for correct answer, otherwise 1 for suitable method.